T0108105

The U.S. Constitution: A Very Short Introduction

VERY SHORT INTRODUCTIONS are for anyone wanting a stimulating and accessible way into a new subject. They are written by experts, and have been translated into more than 45 different languages.

The series began in 1995, and now covers a wide variety of topics in every discipline. The VSI library now contains over 500 volumes—a Very Short Introduction to everything from Psychology and Philosophy of Science to American History and Relativity—and continues to grow in every subject area.

Very Short Introductions available now:

Available soon:

For more information visit our web site

www.oup.com/vsi/

David J. Bodenhamer

THE U.S.
CONSTITUTION

A Very Short Introduction

OXFORD
UNIVERSITY PRESS

OXFORD
UNIVERSITY PRESS

Oxford University Press is a department of the University of Oxford.
It furthers the University's objective of excellence in research, scholarship,
and education by publishing worldwide. Oxford is a registered trademark of
Oxford University Press in the UK and certain other countries.

Published in the United States of America by Oxford University Press
198 Madison Avenue, New York, NY 10016, United States of America.

Library of Congress Cataloging-in-Publication Data
Names: Bodenhamer, David J., author.
Title: The U.S. Constitution : a very short introduction /
David J. Bodenhamer.
Other titles: United States Constitution
Description: New York : Oxford University Press, 2018. | Series: Very short
introductions | Includes bibliographical references and index.
Identifiers: LCCN 2017050024 | ISBN 9780195378320 (paperback)
Subjects: LCSH: Constitutional history—United States. | Constitutional
law—United States. | United States. Constitution. | BISAC: LAW /
Constitutional. | POLITICAL SCIENCE / Constitutions.
Classification: LCC KF4541 .B635 2018 | DDC 342.7302—dc23
LC record available at https://lccn.loc.gov/2017050024

13
Printed in Great Britain
by Ashford Colour Press Ltd., Gosport, Hants.
on acid-free paper

To Raven and Joey, with love

Contents

List of illustrations

Preface

The US Constitution is the world's oldest written constitution, but its impact is as recent as today's news. Claims and counterclaims about the constitutionality of governmental actions are a habit of American politics. Americans repeatedly invoke the Constitution to promote actions they favor and to block actions they oppose. This practice has long roots. Alexis de Tocqueville famously observed in the 1830s that in the United States virtually all political questions ultimately become legal questions. One reason lies in the Constitution itself. This document, which its framers designed to restrain power, often has made political conflict inevitable. It also has accommodated and legitimized the inevitable political and social changes of a vibrant, powerful democratic nation.

The Constitution is notably short—4,400 words in its original version, briefer than any other written constitution. In only seven articles, it established a framework for a national government. It allocated carefully prescribed powers among its branches and between national and preexisting state governments, foresaw the addition of new states, and identified a process for amending its terms. Drafted when the United States was a third-rate nation of 4 million residents, the Constitution now serves as a hallowed touchstone for the world's preeminent economic and military power, with a population of 350 million citizens drawn from all corners of the globe.

Veneration of the Constitution began early. Thomas Jefferson, who in 1787 expressed reservations about the document, hailed it two years later as "unquestionably the wisest ever yet presented to men." Textbooks from the early national period claimed divine inspiration for the framers and praised their work as "sacred." Not everyone agreed: abolitionist William Lloyd Garrison called the Constitution a pact with the devil because it countenanced slavery. Yet from its adoption most citizens have echoed the triumphant note voiced by President Calvin Coolidge in the 1920s, "To live under the American Constitution is the greatest political privilege ever given to the human race."

Such praise obscures the profound disagreements we have had about what the Constitution means. It rarely has been out of the teeth of controversy, and disputes about the text surfaced almost immediately. By the early 1790s two leaders of the Revolution, Thomas Jefferson and Alexander Hamilton, both members of President George Washington's cabinet, were quarreling bitterly about the definition of the necessary and proper clause of Article I that grants Congress incidental authority to carry out its delegated powers. Must its meaning be limited to the plain sense of its terms, as Jefferson insisted, to act as a restraint on power? Or could the clause be read expansively, unless limited elsewhere in the text, to allow the new government to act energetically to protect liberty, as Hamilton desired? Such sharp differences led a tavern keeper to complain in 1798 that the Constitution "is made like a Fiddle, with but few Strings, so that the ruling majority could play any tune upon it as they pleased."

Which Constitution—and how well do we know it?

We have had numerous versions of the Constitution. The first one emerged in four distinct stages from 1787 to the early 1790s—the document produced in Philadelphia, the Constitution ratified by voters in 1788, the one amended in 1791, and the Constitution-in-practice, as the newly formed national government decided what powers the Constitution allowed it to exercise. The Reconstruction amendments created what scholars have deemed the second American Constitution. In fact, each generation has produced a different Constitution, at least interpretively, as the nation responded to changing circumstances.

Even if we did agree on what the document means or on which Constitution Americans venerate, it should not obscure the many attempts to change it. Since its adoption, there have been more than 10,000 efforts to amend the Constitution, and by 2017, twenty-eight states (out of a required thirty-four) had passed resolutions calling for a new constitutional convention. It appears that Americans do not view the document to be as sacrosanct as their rhetoric about it suggests.

Citizens often do not know what the Constitution says, a problem shared by all texts deemed sacred. Surveys have consistently revealed that Americans lack basic knowledge about the nation's fundamental law and even disagree with some of its central tenets, especially when these principles are presented separately. A national poll in 2014 reported that 29 percent of respondents could not name any one of the five guarantees of the First Amendment; other recent polls found that 51 percent erroneously believed the Constitution established a Christian nation and that 22 percent believed that freedom of religion should not apply to extremist groups. In brief, Americans revere a document that many have not read and that they may not endorse in its separate provisions.

Conflicting interpretations

How then should we understand the Constitution? The US Supreme Court asserts that we must accept its interpretation. A 1958 Little Rock desegregation case unanimously declared that its decisions were the "supreme law of the land." Yet this demand at times seems more rhetorical than real. Efforts to blunt or evade civil rights decisions, mostly in southern states, were common in the 1950s and 1960s. Campaigns to repeal or restrict *Roe v. Wade* (1972), the landmark case that affirmed a woman's right to abortion, are continuous. More recently, perceived threats to religious liberty have brought similar challenges, with a presidential candidate in 2016 vowing that the Supreme Court "isn't the Supreme Being." In response to the Court's gay marriage decision in 2015, a US senator argued, "There is no obligation on others in government to accept the court as the final arbiter of every constitutional question."

Accepting the Court as the ultimate arbiter does not resolve the dilemma because sharp divisions exist among the justices themselves about standards of interpretation. In a closely divided Court, a shift by one or two justices often holds the potential for changing what the Constitution requires on any given issue. Today this debate centers on whether ratification fixed the meaning of constitutional text or whether judges can use its principles to fit the document to modern circumstances.

For decades, the terms strict construction or loose construction described the poles of constitutional interpretation. Today we use originalism or the living constitution. Originalism seeks to settle all constitutional questions by reference to the common meaning the text had when ratified. Closely allied to originalism is textualism, initially applied to statutory interpretation, which expects judges to read words in their most ordinary way, without reference to other sources. A popular version of originalism, sometimes called original intent, focuses more on the aims of the framers; the 2010 Pledge to America, a Republican campaign document, promised "to honor the Constitution as constructed by its framers and honor the original intent of those precepts." These views project the belief that judges must reflect the meaning the document had for those who ratified it; under this standard, ratification is the only legitimate expression of the people's will, the trump card in any constitutional matter. Most notably associated with Justice

Antonin Scalia (served 1986–2016), originalism insists on strict construction to restrain unelected judges from writing their own views into the Constitution.

The "living Constitution" holds that judges are obligated to reach decisions in line with the values and principles embraced by the document. They are not free to substitute their own judgment on matters before them but rather are to weigh carefully what outcome is most consistent with the Constitution. In this sense, the document's meaning evolves in a manner analogous to the common law—slowly and incrementally, using precedent to guide the application of constitutional values to new situations. Or as Justice William Brennan (served 1956–1990) wrote, "The ultimate question must be: what do the words of the text mean for our time."

Public opinion on how to interpret the Constitution is evenly divided. A poll in 2014 found that about half of the public (49 percent) believe the Supreme Court should be based on what the Constitution "means in current times," while roughly as many (46 percent) say decisions should be based on what the Constitution "meant as it was originally written." In our hyper-partisan age, Republicans and Democrats have sharply different views on this question. Almost 70 percent of Republicans want the justices to hew to the original meaning, while the same percentage of Democrats favor decisions that adapt the Constitution to modern times.

An appeal to the historical record cannot resolve this debate. Evidence from the Constitutional Convention is too limited— and from the ratification debates too contradictory—to provide convincing proof of a given reading. A surer standard is to recognize the problems the framers were trying to solve, as well as the values and ideas that influenced their choices. Here the record is more complete; we have ample evidence of the circumstances that gave rise to the Constitution, which came at a point when revolutionary leaders had become anxious about whether the nation they had created could survive. Understanding the Constitution requires that we understand how and why it was created. Only then will we be able to explore how the founders' vision has played out across the course of American history.

Chapter 1
The revolutionary Constitution

The American Revolution was a radical event that redefined ideas of sovereignty, liberty, equality, representation, and power. It also recast how men and women related to each other within and outside of government. As its political expression, the Constitution was the revolutionary answer to an age-old antagonism in Western culture between power and liberty. James Madison, who shaped our understanding of it more than any other founder, wrote, "Every word of the [Constitution] decides a question between power and liberty." What made the American experience unique, he continued, was its answer: "In Europe, charters of liberty have been granted by power. America has set the example...of charters of power decided by liberty."

The Revolution began as a constitutional argument about the rights of Englishmen who had migrated to the New World. The slogan "no taxation without representation" was not about taxes but about the right to meaningful representation. Other constitutional arguments soon followed: How far did parliamentary power extend? How could rights be secured against abuses of British power? Ultimately the colonists concluded that their liberty required independence. They ceased asserting their rights as Englishmen and in the Declaration of Independence claimed rights that were universal laws of nature. Yet independence itself raised an important constitutional question: What form of government would best protect rights and secure liberty?

Revolutionary republicanism

American revolutionaries believed that power and liberty were intractable foes; the only way to protect liberty was to restrain power. For them, power in government—always rapacious and always a danger to liberty—was the central problem posed by independence. From their study of history, they concluded that only a republic satisfied the need to grant government sufficient power to provide security without threatening liberty. From the Latin *res publica*, or public affairs, a republic acted in the people's interests because it rested firmly on popular consent, which, as seventeenth-century English political theorist John Locke had argued, was the proper basis for government. Popular consent limited the power government could exercise.

Republics made men citizens capable of self-government rather than subjects to be governed. The difference between subjects and citizens was immense, noted David Ramsey, a South Carolina physician and historian: "Subjects look up to a master, but citizens are so far equal that none have hereditary rights superior to others." In a world in which class and status were birthrights, this belief in the equality of citizens was radical. By overthrowing monarchy and establishing republics, an ideal if elusive form of self-government, Americans would redeem Thomas Paine's boast that they "had the power to begin the world over again." Republics would foster a radical experiment in liberty by empowering citizens and restraining the reach of government.

History provided examples of successful republics in ancient Greece and Rome, but it also had revealed them to be fragile. This form of government required much of its citizens, who had a duty to pursue the public good instead of their own self-interest. They also had to choose wise men to govern them. Above all, republican citizens must remain united in the face of monarchies that would seek their destruction. The need for unity meant that republics could exist only in geographically small and socially homogeneous areas, certainly nothing larger than the new states.

Such requirements were challenging. Americans not only lived in one of the most diverse societies the world had known, but also they understood that people were naturally self-interested. Yet if republics demanded much from individuals, they promised greater liberty. This prize persuaded Americans to undertake their quest to reinvent government. If successful, the revolutionaries believed that a new citizenry would emerge, one filled with public virtue and capable of defending the rights of men.

Limited government, popular consent, public virtue, and political equality characterized a republic; they were not a road map for forming one. The need, as the Continental Congress directed, was for the thirteen colonies to organize themselves into states based on the "authority of the people." Within days after declaring independence, state legislatures transformed colonial governments into republican ones through the adoption of written constitutions that prescribed what powers the government could exercise. This innovation became central to American constitutionalism. It was a radical step because constitutions traditionally followed the practices of government rather than restrained them. The British constitution, for instance, had no fixed form; it vested sovereignty in Parliament and incorporated its acts, along with ancient laws such as Magna Carta, into an organic, or dynamic, constitution. A written constitution restricted what government could do.

State constitutions limited power in a variety of ways. They rejected the British theory of mixed government in favor of separation of powers. The British constitution had blended three forms of government—monarchy, aristocracy, and democracy, each corresponding to classes in the social order—into a unitary government. The revolutionaries instead divided the functions of government—executive, legislative, and judicial—into branches without reference to social constituencies. The constitutions vested primary authority in the lower house of the legislature, the one closest to the people, and sharply restrained executive power. Finally, they included a listing of individual rights, including newly discovered ones, that government could not abridge.

Despite the initial success of state-making, a significant constitutional problem remained. Republics relied on popular consent, yet the new state charters were creations of legislatures that had been colonial one day and independent the next. How had the people given consent? This question became increasingly important because the Revolution advanced a new conception of sovereignty—popular sovereignty. English tradition focused on the act of creating government, with the people giving up their authority to rulers who would protect their rights. The revolutionaries embraced the radical idea that people retained ultimate authority and gave government limited power for defined purposes. But how did the people as a body agree to what government could do on their behalf?

Massachusetts solved this problem in 1780 with a constitutional convention. Only a body chosen separately by voters for the sole purpose of writing a fundamental charter—and whose work must be approved by voters—could act with the people's consent. The constitutional convention and ratification process, both innovations, made it possible to distinguish popular sovereignty from governmental sovereignty and fundamental law from ordinary law. Ratification also established the supremacy of constitutional law, which alone reflected the abiding will of the people.

Written constitutions, bills of rights, constitutional conventions, popular sovereignty, and the supremacy of fundamental law were important developments that shaped American constitutionalism. Each one advanced the republican state, which should have led to

4

an increase in liberty and public virtue. Events soon demonstrated that these steps were not enough to promote or protect revolutionary ends.

The crisis of the Revolution

By the early 1780s, a new problem, democracy, put republicanism in peril. Everywhere people pursued their self-interest at the expense of the common good. State legislatures enacted laws that benefited a majority but endangered the rights of minorities; later characterized as tyranny of the majority, republican theory did not imagine this outcome. Westerners fought with easterners about the adequacy of protection provided for their lives and property. Religious rights were at risk by taxing all citizens to support established churches that were vestiges from the colonial period. Property rights were especially vulnerable, as debtors sought relief from creditors. The threat to property was troubling because experience taught that it was the "guardian of every other right."

Such factious politics distressed revolutionary leaders, who had counted on public virtue to ensure the success of republicanism. They never imagined that the people could be the source of tyranny: "An elective despotism was not the government we fought for," wrote Thomas Jefferson in 1784. The Revolution, in fact, had reshaped society as well as government. The rise of democratic politics confounded a republican assumption that both political equality and deference to the rule of wise men were required for a stable society.

Whether the nation could succeed was also in doubt, as thirteen separate republics pulled in their own directions to the exclusion of a larger national purpose. States taxed the commerce of other states to protect their own manufacturers and merchants. The weak national government, established in 1783 under the Articles of Confederation, was powerless to intervene. Described as a "league of friendship" among the states, it lacked authority. The

Confederation could not tax or enforce its own laws, regulate commerce among the states, or provide security. Ironically, it was ineffective for a reason on which all revolutionary republicans agreed: centralized power was the greatest threat to liberty.

Americans divided sharply over what had gone wrong. A significant number blamed democratic state legislatures. Commercially minded revolutionaries, such as merchants and planters, believed that narrow parochial interests—and too much democracy—posed a barrier to union or, more pointedly, a national market. Other revolutionaries disagreed with this diagnosis. For them, state legislatures were not democratic enough; they were captive of special interests and did not represent the people. The war debt had resulted in a tax burden that, for most Americans, was higher than the one they had experienced under the British and fell unevenly on farmers. In one instance in 1786—Shays's Rebellion—unrest became armed resistance as farmers stormed the courthouse in Springfield, Massachusetts, to prevent foreclosure on their land.

Shays's Rebellion brought the crisis of revolutionary republicanism to its head. Using a well-settled approach, Virginia invited the states to a convention in Annapolis, Maryland, to address the inability of the Confederation Congress to settle commercial disputes. The delegates instead called for a new effort to remedy the Confederation's defects. The gathering in Philadelphia on May 25, 1787, that would produce the US Constitution was a response to this call.

The Philadelphia convention

The Constitutional Convention developed the structure of government that we recognize today. It tackled the problems of republicanism that plagued the founding generation, but it did not abandon the Revolution. The framers instead reached pragmatic compromises that built upon the advances of the previous decade. In the process, they would make innovations in republicanism that allowed it to embrace an increasingly democratic future.

The fifty-five delegates from twelve states (Rhode Island did not participate) were, as John Adams characterized them, men of "Ability, Weight, and Experience" whose perspective was cosmopolitan, not provincial. Most delegates were wealthy; twenty-five were slave owners; forty-two had served in the Continental Congress. They sought to fashion a strong yet restrained national government that did not depend on virtuous people. The absence of republicans who did not share their goals—Samuel Adams, Thomas Jefferson, and Patrick Henry, among others—made their job easier. It also raised suspicions among a wary public that the convention's work offered insufficient protection for their hard-won liberty.

Even though delegates agreed on the need to strengthen national authority, divisions existed among them. Members from large, commercially minded states desired a central government strong enough to corral excess democracy and rein in states that followed their self-interest at the expense of the nation. They also wanted an active government to foster a national market and promote commerce and manufacturing. Delegates from smaller, agricultural states worried more about the potential of centralized power to threaten liberty. Slavery was another fault line. Southerners feared the danger that a strong central government posed for their property rights in slave labor. These differences meant that any agreements necessarily would involve compromise.

The delegates wrestled over questions of power and structure. How could they create a central government capable of addressing the nation's ills without weakening states, the governments most trusted by citizens, or without making national authority dependent on states, the plague of the Articles of Confederation?

How would they allocate power to avoid an overweening legislature or a too-strong executive? Could they create an energetic government without jeopardizing the rights of citizens? Could they remain true to republican principles?

James Madison, who kept the most complete record of the proceedings, provided intellectual leadership. To address the problems of republicanism, he proposed a strong national government with representation based on population. It could veto state legislation as well as tax and enforce its own laws directly. To prevent the abuse of power, authority would be divided and balanced among branches of the government. Embodied in the Virginia Plan, or large-state plan, it was a bold vision with majority support, 7-1, from the voting states. Yet many details were uncertain, and every question about form raised a concern about power.

The longer the debate continued, the greater the unease among delegates from smaller states. They worried that proportional representation would lead to a tyranny of large states over small ones. They also were not convinced that a national government could be republican. Their solution was the New Jersey Plan, which sought only to revise the Articles of Confederation, thereby maintaining state sovereignty. It made several concessions, notably allowing the national government to tax citizens directly and accepting the supremacy of national law. Yet small-state advocates were not willing to consign the states to a meaningless role. What entity besides republican states could represent the interests of the people and protect their liberty?

The New Jersey Plan failed, 7-3, but the small states remained firm in their opposition to the Virginia Plan. A long stalemate followed. The choices were too stark: the union was to be either a sovereign national government or a federation of sovereign state governments. Rufus King of Massachusetts suggested a way out of the dilemma. Why, he asked, did sovereignty have to reside in one government? What if it were divided between governments? This solution was possible because popular sovereignty allowed the people to assign governmental power in whatever manner they chose.

King's question was catalytic, and the delegates quickly sought to reconcile the two plans. They settled on divided sovereignty or federalism, a term increasingly defined as a system of shared power rather than a federation of sovereign states. The phrase "national government" in the Virginia Plan became simply "the government of the United States," a symbolically important shift. The New Jersey Plan's requirement that state courts enforce national law was more suited to the new meaning of federalism than was the Virginia Plan's proposal for a national veto of state law, especially when linked to a provision that made national law and treaty obligations supreme.

In the Great (or Connecticut) Compromise, one house of the Congress of the United States, the House of Representatives, would be proportioned by population and directly elected by districts, while the Senate would represent the states equally, with each state allotted two senators chosen by popularly elected state legislatures. (The 17th Amendment, passed in 1913, provided for direct election of senators.) Significantly, Congress no longer rested on the consent of the states, as it had under the Articles; it now reflected the people's will directly and could be trusted with the authority belonging to a national government, especially the power to tax and regulate commerce.

This compromise, however, raised another issue—how to count slaves. Slaves were valuable property, and southerners feared that excluding them from the basis for representation would allow the more populous northern states to tax them. Northerners wanted to restrict representation to free people only. The three-fifths compromise provided an answer, with three slaves counted as the equivalent of five white persons for purposes of representation in

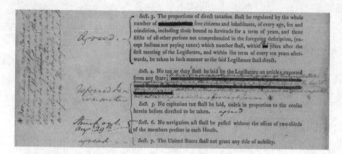

1. In his personal copy of a draft of the Constitution, George Washington handwrote the compromises that the delegates made regarding slavery. These also included a ban on the import of slaves after 1808, and the required return of fugitive slaves to their owners.

the lower house and for taxation. Another compromise forbade taxes on exports, a desire of northern states, and limited any import duties on slaves, as well as barred interference with the slave trade for twenty years after ratification.

Antislavery advocates in the mid-nineteenth century condemned these compromises, but they were neither explicit endorsements of racial hierarchy nor forerunners of a militant pro-slavery ideology. They were instead an answer to the convention's continuing struggle to define important governmental functions, especially to protect rights in property and to distribute and balance power fairly. Nonetheless, it was clear that blacks at best existed only on the margins of this new republican order.

The last major hurdle involved the structure and role of the executive branch. As the embodiment of popular sovereignty, Congress was to be the great engine of government, but the separation of powers principle required a counterweight to its broad authority. Was it possible to create a strong chief executive without feeding the human tendency to abuse power? Also, popular sovereignty implied election by the people, but how—directly or indirectly? Would the people know enough about the candidates to choose wisely? The fear that an electorate would chose a heroic figure who had no other qualification for office kept most delegates from seriously considering direct election.

The compromise reached in early September proposed a president chosen by indirect election. States would have electors equal to their representation in Congress who would cast individual votes for the two people they considered the best qualified to serve as president and vice president. The Electoral College—the name became official in 1845—made possible a relationship between the president and the nation, unlike Congress whose members represented local districts or states only. In time, the president would become the unrivaled symbol and executor of the national will.

The draft presented for approval on September 12 was a prosaic document that had none of the soaring language of the Declaration of Independence. It was the product of long debates and countless concessions that led to positions no one proposed initially. But compromise did not mean an abandonment of principle or purpose. The framers faced a crisis of confidence in republican government: the Revolution failed to produce citizens filled with concern for the public good. The new Constitution allowed imperfect citizens to govern themselves by carefully dividing and balancing governmental authority. For the delegates, this system of restraints best protected their hard-won liberty.

The framers' Constitution

All twelve state delegations and thirty-nine members signed the proposed constitution. Its first three articles, on the legislative, executive, and judicial branches respectively, outlined a deliberate hierarchy, with the legislature assuming first rank. The remaining four articles dealt with a variety of subjects, including the relationships among the states (IV), the process for amendments (V), the supremacy of the Constitution (VI), and the ratification process (VII). A preamble, initially conceived as a list of the states, became instead a statement of purpose, proclaimed in the name of the people of the United States. Although without any legal force—it neither grants nor restricts authority—this opening paragraph announced that the sovereign people were vesting power in government for certain, specified ends.

The proposed constitution divided power among three separate branches of government and between the central government and the states. Article I addressed the make-up, election, and powers of Congress, a bicameral (two-house) body with each branch chosen differently. The House, with members elected by districts, had one exclusive power—impeachment (an accusation of misconduct)—and one power it had to exercise first—all revenue bills had to begin in the lower chamber. Elected by state legislatures, the Senate was indirectly representative of the people and served as a brake on the House's democratic tendencies, with a minimum age (thirty years, greater by five years) and a longer term for its members (six years instead of two). It had the exclusive power of approval ("advise and consent") for presidential appointments.

Acting as Congress, the two branches possessed seventeen categories of specific powers, detailed in Section 8; the most important, the power to tax and to regulate interstate commerce, addressed problems under the Confederation. Section 9 contained eight clauses denying Congress the power to act: for example, it could not suspend the writ of habeas corpus except for invasion or rebellion, make ex post facto laws, or pass export taxes. Section 10 prohibited the states from infringing the powers of Congress in matters of taxation, war, and diplomacy. Otherwise, the states could exercise whatever powers their respective constitutions permitted.

Article II created the executive branch in brief language that is both precise and frustratingly vague. It began with a simple declaratory sentence: "The executive Power shall be vested in a President of the United States." It differed from Article I, which referred to "legislative powers herein granted." Did the framers recognize inherent executive powers while granting only restricted authority to Congress? Presidents since Washington have made this claim. In doing so they have relied as well on the prescribed oath of office to "faithfully execute the Office of the President of the United States and…preserve, protect and defend the Constitution…."

The article outlined specific duties and obligations of the president, many of which mimicked royal prerogatives. He was commander-in-chief of the armed forces, had to assent to legislation and could veto bills (a power granted in Article I), appointed federal officeholders and judges, could make treaties, and had the power to pardon. Republican concerns did not permit a grant of unrestrained authority, however. Congress could override a veto by a two-thirds vote in both houses, and treaties and appointments to office required the advice and consent of two-thirds of the Senate. The president had to report periodically to Congress on the state of the union. Nowhere did the document outline the president's war powers, but here too there were limits and a division of authority—Congress had the power to declare war, appropriate money, and establish rules for the military; the president was commander-in-chief—that soon became a subject of heated and continuing debate. The article also permitted removal of a president or vice president for "high crimes and misdemeanors" by impeachment in the House and conviction by the Senate.

Article III on the judiciary was briefer and more general but it too rested on republican assumptions. In Britain, dispensing justice was a royal obligation. The Constitution created a separate and equal branch, with federal judges holding office indefinitely on "good behavior," which insulated them from popular passions. It also set the stage for judicial review by extending authority to decide all cases arising under the Constitution and the laws and treaties of the United States, including disputes between states and citizens of different states. (The Constitution grants no advisory power to the judiciary.) The Supreme Court had limited original jurisdiction, however, and generally could exercise its power only on appeal. Other provisions required a jury trial for all crimes except impeachment and strictly defined the terms of treason to prevent its prosecution for political ends.

The article was either mute or sketchy on such matters as how many justices would sit on the Supreme Court, how many lower courts would exist, or what would be the extent of their appellate authority. All these decisions were left to Congress, which provided the basic structure for the federal courts in the Judiciary Act of 1789, passed during its first session. What was certain, however, was the ability of the new government to enforce national law through its own courts, as the Confederation could not.

Article IV included the principle of reciprocity (or comity): states had to give "full faith and credit" to the acts, records, and proceedings of other states; the citizens of each state would have "all privileges and immunities" of citizens of other states; states were bound to return escaped prisoners and slaves to states from which they had fled. The aim of these specific provisions was clear—the Constitution created a singular United States, with equal (but undefined) citizenship, although initially for free persons only. A separate clause provided for admission of new states on terms equal to existing states, thereby rejecting an empire. Section 4 guaranteed to each state a "Republican Form of Government," although it provided no definition of one.

Articles V and VI also reflected the lessons of revolutionary government under the Confederation. The amendment process became somewhat less onerous, requiring a supermajority rather than unanimity to change the Constitution (Article V). National law and treaties were supreme over state law, including state constitutions, with state courts required to enforce federal law (Article VI). Other provisions prohibited religious tests for public office (Article VI), the only mention of religion in this secular document. The final article (VII) set the terms for ratification, with nine states required to affirm the new charter before it took effect.

Ratification

When state conventions met to ratify the Constitution, their delegates debated a document that offered a mechanical solution to the problem of governmental power, one suited to the age of scientific enlightenment. Just as Deists imagined God as a master watchmaker, devising a universe that ran on its own internal rules, so the framers believed that the right architecture for government would allow imperfect men to govern themselves. The structure of government would correct what the weakness of men could not. In their "new order for the ages," the framers reflected a central lesson from the 1780s: unalloyed governmental power, even when entrusted to the people's representatives, was dangerous. The only sure way to trust power was to divide and restrain it; however, properly limited, a strong, energetic national government would preserve the liberty gained by the Revolution.

Not everyone agreed. Opponents charged that the framers had betrayed the Revolution, and they mounted attacks that questioned the framers' motives. Farmers, artisans, and backcountry settlers, many from small states, were suspicious that the ambitious, commercially minded men from large states wanted a government powerful enough to advance their selfish interests and to subvert the rising democracy unleashed by the Revolution.

Alarmed by the voices raised against ratification, proponents of a strong national government sought to persuade Americans of the proposed constitution's virtues. A series of eighty-five newspaper essays—collectively known as *The Federalist*, written by Alexander

Hamilton, James Madison, and John Jay (later the first chief justice of the United States)—defended the document by exploring how the new government would work. They also explained how it satisfied republican theory.

The Federalist argued that the proposed constitution embodied a new understanding of sovereignty. As ultimate authority, the people made an explicit grant of delegated powers to the government, which protected liberty by preventing government from acting in areas the people had not authorized. The constitution also made the central government representative of the people, both directly and indirectly. This extension of the representative principle to the national government had two important implications. The central government could enforce its own laws on the people, whose representatives had given their consent. It also created a national republic.

The notion of a national republic, previously considered a self-contradictory term, required a new understanding of republican theory. Under the classical conception, factions, or special interests, undermined the unity that republics required to survive. In *Federalist 10*, James Madison argued that experience had demonstrated the folly of trusting unity and direct democracy to protect liberty. Legislative majorities in the states, for instance, had weakened minority rights. The solution was to increase the number of interest groups, a consequence of a national republic, thereby making it much more difficult for them to create a permanent majority. A large, diverse republic also expanded the number of candidates for office, making it unlikely that unqualified individuals would win.

Madison conceded that a large republic produced its own problems, such as choosing representatives "too little acquainted with local circumstances," but another structural innovation, federalism, provided a corrective by acknowledging national and state interests alike. Was it possible to have both sufficient diversity to check factions and the commonality required for a nation to exist? Here, John Jay, in *Federalist 2*, reminded readers that America already was "one united people—a people descended from the same ancestors, speaking the same language, professing the same religion." The new nation enjoyed the blessings of both unity and diversity.

Anti-Federalists were not convinced. They operated from an older conception of republicanism: only small, homogeneous republics produced the harmony of interests required for effective government. The wide disparity in economic interests in a national republic was a matter of special concern, with conflict inevitable between northern commerce and southern plantation agriculture. Opponents also remained committed to an earlier view that power and liberty were bitter enemies and that a united citizenry, devoted to the common good, was essential to protect liberty.

Like the Federalists, the Anti-Federalists produced voluminous writings that warned, presciently, about the problems of government under the new constitution. Unlike the *Federalist*, they had no coherent message. Their most consistent theme was the perceived threat to individual liberties. The proposed constitution contained no bill of rights, nor, with few exceptions, did it include any guarantee of the most basic individual liberties. Federalists explained that the constitution granted the central government no power to restrict individual liberties; any power not given to the central government remained with the states or the people. Opponents countered that since the laws of the United States were supreme, state constitutions offered little protection. Without a bill of rights, they argued, government could quickly slide into tyranny.

The lack of a bill of rights placed ratification in jeopardy. Five states already had endorsed the constitution when the Massachusetts ratification convention demanded that a bill of rights be added. Other states followed suit, voting yes but with the same recommendation. When Virginia and New York ratified in June and July 1788, the Constitution was a political and legal reality. So too was the necessity to amend it immediately with a bill of rights.

The amended Constitution

As a newly elected member of the House of Representatives, James Madison assumed responsibility for adding individual rights to the Constitution. Earlier he believed that a declaration of rights would be a "parchment barrier" incapable of protecting liberty; now he concluded that written guarantees would serve as "good ground for an appeal to the sense of community" if states or oppressive majorities threatened liberty. He worried much about majorities running roughshod over the rights of minorities, especially in matters of conscience, and feared states would not be able to resist this kind of tyranny.

Madison initially proposed that the Bill of Rights apply to the states as well as the central government, a condition rejected by Congress because of its implications for state sovereignty. Not until the twentieth century would rights be nationalized in this way and then by the courts, not Congress. This development likely would not have surprised Madison, who believed an independent judiciary, operating through open courts, would "resist every encroachment on rights expressly stipulated for in the constitution" and form an "impenetrable bulwark against every assumption of power in the legislative or executive."

Madison proposed nine amendments to the first congress in 1788; they became twelve amendments when submitted for ratification. By 1791, the states had ratified ten of them, now known as the Bill of Rights. The amendments borrowed heavily from the Virginia Declaration of Rights and the various state bills of rights, all of which stemmed from a mix of English history, colonial experience, and revolutionary ideas. They included two types of guarantees:

rights necessary for representative government, such as freedom of religion, speech, press, and peaceable assembly; and rights of the accused, including protections against double jeopardy and self-incrimination as well as the right to counsel and trial by jury. The Ninth Amendment reserved any unnamed rights to the people, and, to satisfy an Anti-Federalist concern, the Tenth Amendment reserved any unspecified powers to the states or the people.

In what became a pattern of American history, the central role of rights in American constitutional law was due as much, if not more, to the demands of an insistent citizenry as it was to the framers' design. The list of rights was far advanced for its time, but no one believed that its protections benefited American Indians, African Americans, or even white women. Only democratic demands for inclusion would make these rights available to all Americans. Even then, it would take almost two hundred years for them to become truly national.

The revolutionary legacy

With the ratification of the Bill of Rights in 1791, the revolutionary Constitution was complete. It was the product of compromise, and as such it left fundamental questions unaddressed and unanswered. It did not mention equality, even though the Declaration of Independence had included it as one of the nation's ideals. The Constitution rested on popular sovereignty—"We, the people"—yet its practical meaning was ambiguous. It established a representative process but left unaddressed the question of how much power the people had surrendered to government and how much they retained for themselves. The difference mattered because popular sovereignty made the people both rulers and ruled.

From the moment of passage, the powers and rights set forth in the new Constitution came into dispute. The tension between power and liberty did not disappear—if anything, it became stronger—as people grappled with the practical problems of government. Over the next two centuries, the Constitution would be challenged, amended, reinterpreted, circumvented, ignored, and, at times, subverted. It would be a weapon in political and class warfare, its phrases used as cudgels to advance or beat back change. It would be expanded and contracted by court decisions, congressional acts, and presidential orders. Yet it survives, which is testimony to its central role in the nation's continuing experiment in liberty.

The Constitution, so often viewed as a conservative charter, was the product of this revolutionary age. Its framers embraced something they could not have predicted in 1776: power and liberty need not stand in opposition to each other. Power in government, properly structured, could promote and protect liberty. Not everyone agreed. For opponents of the Constitution, perhaps half of the population, power in government remained what it had been throughout history—the enemy of liberty.

Countless clashes between these two views have marked American history. Ironically, both were right. The Constitution was a synthesis. It restrained power on behalf of liberty, but it also granted power to promote and protect liberty. Each decade that followed its adoption would define the meaning of this synthesis— and test whether the Constitution was capable of securing the Revolution's radical experiment in liberty.

Past concerns and experiences have molded the Constitution's meaning in both law and practice. Core constitutional themes— federalism, balance of powers, property, equality, representation, rights, and security—assumed prominence at different times in response to particular political and social conditions. These themes do not exist in isolation from each other—indeed, they frequently overlap—nor do they reflect only the views of the Supreme Court. American constitutionalism is the product of more forces than judicial pronouncements. But these constitutional ideas have shaped American politics and culture, and the demands of a vibrant nation have given new expression to the framer's Constitution. They each reveal how the Constitution has served—and continues to serve—as a revolutionary framework both for legitimating power and for advancing liberty.

Chapter 2
Federalism

Federalism, the division of power between state and central governments, was the most novel doctrine to emerge from the Constitutional Convention. It embraced a contradiction, *imperium in imperio*, a sovereignty within a sovereignty. This logical inconsistency—classical theory assumed that governmental sovereignty was indivisible—could be explained only by another innovation, popular sovereignty, that vested ultimate power in the people.

Federalism has proven to be a highly malleable scheme for accommodating the demands of a diverse society and a dynamic economy. What began in 1787 as a partnership of equal governments became a powerful national government two centuries later, with widespread authority to safeguard (or threaten) liberty for its citizens. Today the morphing of federalism appears inevitable, yet nothing could be further from the truth. Its development was uncertain, and few constitutional issues have been as contentious.

Advocates of states' rights have longed believed that power in a large and distant central government is a menace to liberty. Supporters of a strong national government have argued that authority exercised from a vigorous center advances the cause of liberty. These positions have not tracked neatly or consistently with political ideology, party affiliation, or regional identity, and both sides often have embraced a position they once rejected. During the administration of President Donald Trump, for example, liberals resurrected state sovereignty claims they spurned under the Obama presidency, whereas triumphant conservatives embraced national power they sought to block only a few months earlier. There is no easy symmetry in the history of American federalism.

The demands of an expansive economy, democratic politics, and war have shifted power from states to the central government as people sought advantage for their interests through national action. Proponents of states' rights aided this shift by insisting on state sovereignty to maintain regimes of slavery and segregation or to exclude labor, women, and immigrants from the democratic process. Still, it would be incorrect to conclude that states are irrelevant. In education, criminal justice, public health, and public safety, state and local governments have long been important and, at times, preeminent. They also have been laboratories of democracy, with health-care reform, tax-subsidized economic development, and recognition of same-sex marriage among recent state initiatives. The story of federalism is both a narrative of national power and a counternarrative of local control.

Conflict over the relative power of national and state governments arose early. During the 1790s the United States became entangled in the imperial war between Great Britain and revolutionary France. Jeffersonian Republicans sympathized with the French overthrow of the monarchy, whereas Federalists feared the political radicalism and class conflict it unleashed. The so-called Quasi-War with France (1798–1800) persuaded the Federalist-dominated Congress to pass the controversial Alien and Sedition Acts (1798) that, among other measures, punished criticism of the national government or its officials. Sedition was especially dangerous, Federalists argued, because it undermined the authority and stability of republican government. Within months, eager prosecutors convicted Republican newspaper editors (and one congressman) of sedition despite the First Amendment's guarantees of free speech and free press.

It was an early test of federalism. Republicans viewed the acts as an infringement of freedom of speech but under what authority could they resist? Not until 1803 would the Supreme Court establish its role to declare a national law unconstitutional. Although vindication came when Republicans triumphed in the election of 1800, an appeal to states provided more immediate shelter. Led secretly by Thomas Jefferson, who was vice president, and his friend, James Madison, the Virginia and Kentucky legislatures embraced ideas that in more extreme form justified southern secession decades later.

The Kentucky and Virginia Resolutions claimed that the Constitution resulted from a compact of the states, with each state able to judge whether the central government had acted legally. States could shield citizens from enforcement of what they considered unconstitutional measures (interposition)—and, in extreme cases, they could nullify illegal acts within their borders. No other state embraced the resolutions, but the protests of 1798 and 1799 advanced three ideas—interposition, nullification, and the state compact theory of union—that would prove to be a seedbed for disunion.

The ideas embodied in the Kentucky and Virginia Resolutions did not disappear when the acts expired in 1801. Regional opposition to the War of 1812 led to the Hartford Convention, called by the Federalist remnant in New England to resist a war ruinous to their economic interests. Talk of state sovereignty, interposition, and secession was rife. The compact theory of the union and states' rights had found a new home in the party and region that, twenty years earlier, touted the virtues of an energetic national government.

The war's successful conclusion temporarily discredited states' rights radicalism and marked the end of the Federalist Party. The misnamed Era of Good Feelings (1815–1828) produced a burst of enthusiasm for national action to address weaknesses revealed by the conflict. Jeffersonian Republicans, now the only party, embraced a constitutional nationalism they earlier had rejected, with Congress enacting a protective tariff and chartering a national bank they opposed in the 1790s. Their actions were pragmatic: a national emergency required national power. It was an early riff on a consistent theme in the history of American federalism.

More than Congress, however, the US Supreme Court, led by John Marshall, set the terms of federalism, with national supremacy over the states the hallmark of its jurisprudence. In 1819, the Marshall Court (1801–1835) tackled a case squarely on this issue. Maryland sought to tax all non-state chartered banks operating within its boundaries, which included the Second Bank of the United States. The branch refused to pay on grounds that states lacked authority to tax a congressionally chartered bank. The Marshall Court unanimously agreed, with its ruling in *McCulloch v. Maryland* still the leading decision on the power of the national government. The necessary and proper clause of Article I, Marshall wrote, allowed Congress to act: "Let the end be legitimate, let it be within the scope of the constitution, and all means which are appropriate, which are plainly adapted to that end, which are not prohibited, but consistent with the letter and spirit of the constitution, are constitutional." The supremacy clause also shielded the branch from the state levy, Marshall held, because "the power to tax is the power to destroy."

Other decisions expanded national power, with the Marshall Court declaring state laws unconstitutional on an average of one per year. In one case, it held that the commerce clause granted broad congressional power to regulate interstate commerce; in another, it ruled that a state could not use even its legitimate powers to promote public health and safety, so-called police powers, if they burdened interstate commerce. The contract clause, which forbade states from "impairing the obligation of contracts," also limited state power, the justices concluded, because a national economy could not exist if states changed agreements at their discretion. For the Marshall Court, the national government represented the will of the people, and, within its delegated powers, its authority was unrivaled.

In fact, states were more active agents of political and economic change than was the national government. State governments promoted, subsidized, and steered their economies. The construction of the National Road (1811–1837), also known as the Cumberland Road, that connected the Potomac and Ohio Rivers stands as an almost solitary example before the Civil War of a major, federally funded, economic development project (or internal improvement). Such limited use of national power, however, did not quell worries about its challenge to liberty.

For the antebellum South, the tariff, a tax on imported goods, signified the danger of national power. In 1828 Congress passed a tariff to protect American manufacturing by increasing the price of competing British goods, especially textiles. Southerners protested that the measure benefited the manufacturing North at their expense. It raised the cost of finished goods and led the British to reduce their purchase of cotton from southern planters. But the South's larger concern related to slavery. If the national government could imperil the region's economic well-being, what was to stop it from limiting or abolishing slavery?

Opposition to the tariff of 1828 was led by South Carolina senator and soon-to-be vice president John C. Calhoun, who secretly wrote a 35,000-word *Exposition and Protest* that gave new force to the doctrines of interposition and nullification. The tariff's only legitimate purpose was to generate revenue, he contended, not to protect American industries; Congress also could not favor manufacturing over agriculture. Under these conditions, a state, acting in a popularly elected convention, retained power to "veto" any unconstitutional measure of the central government. It was a provocative argument because Calhoun rested his case not solely on states' rights but on popular sovereignty as well. The states were not acting as states alone but as agents of the people.

Calhoun's claim reminds us of how often Americans appealed to the revolutionary tradition of popular sovereignty when dissenting from the actions of their government. The Virginia and Kentucky Resolutions, the Hartford Convention, and the Nullification Crisis raised questions about how the people created the nation: collectively as states or as an undifferentiated national body? For the slaveholding states, the answer became progressively tilted toward an extreme version of state sovereignty in which each state could nullify what it judged to be an illegitimate national law within its boundaries. By implication, each state also could decide whether to remain in the union.

The Nullification Crisis ended after President Andrew Jackson threatened to use federal troops to enforce national power. (No other state was willing to stand with South Carolina.) Jackson was characteristically blunt: "The Constitution...forms a government not a league...To say that any State may at pleasure secede from the Union is to say that the United States is not a nation." This position was unambiguous, but it also was limited. Jackson expressed a common view that the Constitution established a permanent union but the national government was limited to its delegated powers, strictly construed. It was a stance well suited to the individualistic, market-oriented American society of the 1830s.

The post-Marshall Supreme Court, led by Jacksonian Chief Justice Roger B. Taney (1836–1864), was much friendlier to state rights. A new constitutional doctrine, dual federalism, replaced Marshall's constitutional nationalism: each government, state and

Philadelphia, Feb. 22, 1832.

Should the nullifiers succeed in their views of separation, and the Union be in consequence dissolved, the following will be an appropriate epitaph.

(Anticipation.)

Disunited States, January 1, 1834.

EPITAPH.

HERE,

To the ineffable joy of the Despots, and Friends of Despotism, throughout the world,

and the universal distress and mortification

OF THE FRIENDS OF HUMAN LIBERTY AND HAPPINESS,

LIE THE SHATTERED REMAINS

of the noblest fabric of Government, ever devised by man,

The Constitution of the United States.

The fatal result of its dissolution was chiefly produced,

by the unceasing efforts of some of the most highly gifted men in the U. S. whose labours, for a series of years have had this sinister tendency,

by the most exaggerated statements of the distress

and sufferings of South Carolina,

(unjustly ascribed to the tariffs of duties on imports)

which, whatever they were, arose from the blighting, blasting, withering effects of SLAVERY;

together with the depreciation of the great Staple of the State,

THE INEVITABLE CONSEQUENCE OF OVER-PRODUCTION:

caused, in a great degree, by the depression of the Manufactures of the country, in 1816, 1817, 1818, 1819, 1820 & 1821, for want of the protection of the government,

WITHHELD BY THE MISERABLE TARIFF OF 1816:

which overspread the land

with distress, and wretchedness, and bankruptcy;

and produced in three years more decay and ruin of national prosperity, than a war of equal duration would have done.

It reduced the value of real estate in Pennsylvania in that space of time 100,000,000 of dollars,

and in all the grain-growing states probably $300,000,000.

It drove thousands and tens of thousands of Manufacturers to farming; and thus, by the conversion of customers into rivals,

DEPRESSED AND RUINED A LARGE PORTION OF THE FARMERS,

who " were driven to seek, in the uncultivated forests of the west, that shelter of which they were deprived in their native states."

Numbers of those depressed farmers

devoted themselves to the culture of Cotton;

hence production so far outran consumption, that our export of uplands, which in 1819 was only 80,508,270 lbs.

rose in 1825 to 161,386,582 lbs. and in 1827 to 279,169,217.

2. In response to high import duties in 1828 and 1832, South Carolina embraced a doctrine of nullification in which the state claimed the right to block national laws that harmed its interests. It was a severe test of federalism and national supremacy and raised serious concerns about whether the nation could survive, as a 1832 broadside from Philadelphia demonstrates. President Andrew Jackson threatened to use military force to uphold the Union, and a compromise tariff in 1833 defused the crisis, which scholars have called a prelude to the Civil War that followed three decades later.

national, was supreme in its own sphere, with a bright line between them. The US Supreme Court was an impartial referee, ensuring that state and central governments did not intrude on the other's authority.

This pragmatic rule worked reasonably well in economic matters; the nation's business was too dynamic and diverse for a small central bureaucracy to monitor. On slavery, however, dual federalism was increasingly at odds with public opinion in northern and western states. The "peculiar institution" rested on a denial of liberty and fostered a class society that conflicted sharply with American values of freedom and equality. When the national mood turned against the proslavery position in the late 1850s, slaveholders again picked up the banner of extreme states' rights and nullification. The issue was never about money and power alone. Without the social control provided by slavery, southerners feared their way of life would end in a cataclysm of black insurrection.

Dual sovereignty could not reconcile slavery and freedom, even though the Taney Court tried. Forced to choose, the fractured justices settled on state sovereignty. *Dred Scott v. Sanford* (1857) held that national and state citizenship were separate and distinct; blacks, who were not citizens, had no rights the federal government must protect. Chief Justice Taney went further by denying federal authority over slavery. It was a stance an increasingly anti-slavery northern public would not accept.

Northern victory in the Civil War settled the constitutional crisis by repudiating state sovereignty and a right of secession. It also redefined the basis and terms of the national union. In his first inaugural address, President Abraham Lincoln declared that common experiences, a common culture, and "the mystic chords of memory" unified Americans, who were a national people before the Revolution. The Constitution—created by the people, not the states, he argued—was written *"to form a more perfect Union,"* words that Lincoln italicized in emphasis. The United States was a singular noun, not a plural one.

Here was a different understanding of federalism: the national government, exercising the people's authority, represented the nation completely; its power was full and unrivaled. Reconstruction policies sought to make this new meaning part of the nation's fundamental law. Three amendments to the Constitution aimed to improve the union by realizing the promise of equality before the law. The Thirteenth Amendment abolished slavery, the Fourteenth Amendment defined citizenship, and the Fifteenth Amendment expanded political participation to freedmen. The Fourteenth Amendment was especially important. It made every person born in the United States both a citizen of their state and a citizen of the nation, with "equal protection of the laws" and "due process of law" guaranteed for all citizens. Previously, Americans were independently citizens of their states and of the United States, with most people looking to state constitutions for the protection of their rights. Had this understanding continued, newly freed African Americans would be vulnerable to abuse, as in fact occurred in 1866 when reconstituted southern states passed "black codes" to deprive ex-slaves of most rights.

Although the Fourteenth Amendment made the national government responsible for protecting the rights of citizens, few people believed that the amendment changed the system of dual sovereignty. Even Congress intended for it to restore federalism, not restructure it. Reconstruction extended the meaning of liberty but it did not lessen the traditional concern about power. Its congressional architects trusted that access to the ballot by blacks would result in state governments protective of their rights, with the federal government intervening only if states failed to do so.

It was a misplaced assumption: with few exceptions, the Court accepted local standards and state differences in the rights of citizens. When butchers in New Orleans claimed that a law requiring them to use a central slaughterhouse violated their Fourteenth Amendment right to work freely in their occupation, the justices drew a sharp distinction between state rights and national rights. States could regulate the conditions of employment as part of their traditional power to protect the health and welfare of their citizens. The Fourteenth Amendment protected only a limited set of national rights (*Slaughterhouse Cases, 1873*).

Subsequent decisions narrowed the list of protected national rights. In 1884, the Court affirmed the pre–Civil War understanding that the Bill of Rights did not apply to the state governments, effectively limiting the rights Congress could protect against state action. The year before the justices held that the Fourteenth Amendment protected individuals against the actions of state government, not against private discrimination. It was a short step to *Plessy v. Ferguson* (1896), which made "separate but equal" treatment permissible, thereby legitimizing widespread racial segregation.

Dual federalism was acceptable for social regulation but it was too messy for large-scale industrialization. The Fourteenth Amendment took on new life as a check on the power of states to govern economic activity. The Supreme Court defined corporations as persons in 1886, which provided them protection against arbitrary state action under the amendment's due process clause. The same year it voided an Illinois law fixing railroad rates as an interference with congressional power over interstate commerce. Congress responded by creating the Interstate Commerce Commission (1887), a regulatory body charged with ensuring reasonable rates. The national government, first by judicial decision and then by statute, had begun to deprive states of authority to regulate the economy.

This new order brought its own problems. Corporate corruption convinced citizens that monopolies posed a greater threat to liberty than did government. This belief changed the debate about federalism. No single state or even groups of states could regulate the new industrial giants, so the only option was to increase national authority to control private power. The Sixteenth Amendment (1913), which authorized a national income tax, made this change possible. With the revenues to create a strong national bureaucracy, the calculus of power began to shift.

The twentieth century expanded national power to respond to economic crises and threats to national security. World War I brought an unprecedented use of centralized power, which served as precedent for the New Deal's response to the Great Depression. It also raised an important constitutional question. Did the national government have the power to interfere in the economy to whatever extent required to stave off financial collapse? At first the Court balked at abandoning traditional restraints but soon the justices retreated. Economic crisis left the Court little choice but to allow national power to save capitalism.

After the mid-1930s, few restraints existed on the ability of the national government to regulate the economy. Federal power under the commerce clause reached virtually all economic activity, a result that echoed Marshall's constitutional nationalism a century earlier. The Court also declared that Congress, not the judiciary, had the final say on whether the regulation was reasonable. Only the voters could check its power.

Soon a wide array of laws and regulations defined activities as within the "stream of commerce" and therefore subject to national authority. In the Civil Rights Act of 1964, for example, Congress relied on the commerce clause rather than the equal protection clause of the Fourteenth Amendment to ban discrimination in public accommodations. Not until 1995 did the Court limit this blanket authority in state-federal conflicts by deciding that regulation of handguns on school property was too far removed from commerce to limit the states' traditional police powers.

Since the late 1980s the Supreme Court has been more assertive in seeking to rebalance federalism by citing the Tenth Amendment, for example, when it declared that Congress could not command state officers to enforce the provisions of a federal gun control law. Although limiting congressional power, such decisions do not auger a return to dual federalism. It is too impractical. States have not clamored for change because they now rely on federal funds to solve increasingly complex problems. Education, crime, economic development, immigration, public health, and a host of other issues have local expressions but few people argue seriously that any state could solve them alone. Only the national government has authority and resources to address issues that transcend state boundaries.

The result is cooperative federalism, with the national and state governments working in partnership to solve problems in a complex, highly diverse society. This version of divided government may not have been foreseen by the framers, but it would not have surprised them. In *Federalist 34*, Alexander Hamilton predicted that the centralizing impact of war and economic crisis would restrict the power of the states to a "very narrow compass" while the demand for national solutions would prove "altogether unlimited."

In another area, individual liberties, the constitutional tide also ran against the states. Beginning in 1896 the Supreme Court extended the due process protection of the Fourteenth Amendment as a restriction on state action by redefining due process to mean a fair result, not simply fair procedures. Known as substantive due process, this concept made judges, not legislatures, the guardian of rights, even though federal courts used it initially to declare state regulation of corporate monopolies unreasonable. By the mid-1920s, however, the Supreme Court included the First Amendment rights of speech and press as a fundamental right protected by the due process clause of the Fourteenth Amendment. Soon rights of the accused were included, as case after case revealed the states' too-casual protection for individual liberties, especially for African Americans, labor unions, and political dissenters.

This nationalization of the Bill of Rights became almost complete by the end of the 1960s, as the Warren Court (1953–1969) incorporated many rights into the due process clause. Such a sharp departure from traditional American federalism spurred politicians to promise to restore state control, but later courts only trimmed, not reversed, the controversial decisions. Too many instances of injustice had caused citizens to look for protection from the national government rather than from their states.

States' rights has lost much of its heft as a constitutional doctrine. A succession of southern governors sought to resurrect it during the 1950s and early 1960s to defeat desegregation, but their use of it was little more than political theater. More recently, state attorneys general tried to block national policies on health care and immigration, with little success. States are not powerless, however. Equal representation in the Senate allows states to influence, impede, and, at times, frustrate national policies, as southern senators did when they filibustered civil rights measures. These tactics were enlisted in an unworthy cause, but their use signaled an important shift in the practice of federalism. It finally had become a matter of ordinary politics.

Ultimately, federalism changed not because of fundamental shifts in doctrine but because the nation changed. National power grew in response to democratic choices and global challenges. Citizens demanded a national response to problems of the elderly, the poor, and the handicapped; they marched for national enforcement of civil rights laws; they lobbied for consumer and environmental protections; and they supported national science, education, and industrial policies vigorous enough to protect American leadership globally. Significantly, advocates for an increased national role have come from both major parties.

Even as national power grows, states continue to have meaningful roles in a wide array of matters affecting the health and welfare of their citizens. Federal courts will be sensitive to the policies and practices of the states in determining when a national consensus exists to justify a reinterpretation of law. Congress cannot ignore the wishes of states because its members reflect state and local constituencies. Americans will insist on this result because they are uncomfortable as a matter of history and preference with government that lacks a local face.

Questions remain about whether national power is too great and whether it is time to restore authority to the states. This debate is one constant in the changing meaning of federalism. Americans continue to search for the right balance of power and liberty. The revolutionary mantra of divided power remains central to this search, as does the framers' bet that power vested in central government, with proper limits, furthers the growth of liberty. It is this original gamble that continues to give life to federalism itself.

Chapter 3
Balance of powers

Dividing power among the branches of government was much easier for the framers to conceptualize than to achieve. Two questions guided them: What were the limits and purposes of national power? What were the roles and responsibilities of the various branches in exercising the government's authority?

No single event resolved these questions, as the Civil War did for matters of federalism. Each branch has made large claims of power; each has experienced stinging rebuffs to those claims. Our modern focus on the judiciary obscures the demands for power in the other branches. The authority of the executive especially has undergone such expansion that observers worry about the rise of an imperial presidency. Earlier, Congress appeared too dominant. Every generation has debated the nature, legitimacy, and locus of governmental power. One lesson is that the revolutionary fear of power and its proposed solution of balance has never died but has taken on new dress.

For all its careful delegation and denial of authority, the Constitution contains language that grants power more generally. Section 8 begins with an elastic clause, "Congress shall have Power to ... provide for the common Defence [sic] and general Welfare of the United States," and it ends with a provision allowing Congress "To make all Laws which shall be necessary and proper" for carrying out its delegated powers. Much of the expansion of national authority has occurred by reference to these general grants of power.

Even as the nation focused on federalism, a struggle involving the balance of power also occupied the central government. In it, the Supreme Court and the president seized opportunities to define their own constitutional powers as equal to Congress. The justices scored an early victory in a *Marbury v. Madison* (1803), a seminal case that confirmed the principle of judicial review.

The Supreme Court had declared a state law unconstitutional in 1796 when it voided a Virginia statute that conflicted with the treaty ending the war with Great Britain. Left unclear was whether the Court could review acts of Congress. In 1801, the lame-duck Federalist government created new courts, but then-secretary of state John Marshall failed to deliver commissions to four new justices of the peace for the District of Columbia before the newly elected Republican Congress repealed the law. An appointee, William Marbury, petitioned the Supreme Court to compel the new secretary of state, James Madison, to deliver his commission.

It was a no-win situation for Marshall, who was now Chief Justice Marshall and who had no independent power to force Madison to act. His solution was Delphic: the justices could not compel delivery because the statute on which Marbury relied was unconstitutional. The Constitution granted the Court original jurisdiction in certain matters only; all other cases had to come to it on appeal. The Judiciary Act of 1789, which created the court system, improperly extended this authority. Marshall's politically shrewd decision established the principle of judicial review of congressional acts and protected the Court from partisan backlash. It also confirmed the Court as a separate but equal branch of the central government.

For much of the nineteenth century, the justices used their authority to develop federal law, especially in commerce and contract, areas in which the Constitution's grant of power was unambiguous. In a diverse and partisan republic, a stable legislative consensus was not always possible, so federal courts settled questions that Congress could not resolve. This stance worked well in commerce, but it also invited the nation's highest court to address the question of slavery in the *Dred Scott v. Sandford* case, with disastrous consequences.

The Civil War and Reconstruction, except for Lincoln's wartime actions, was a period of legislative dominance, until corruption and incompetence eroded public trust in Congress. Without a strong presidency—and with a succession of weak incumbents—the Court filled the vacuum of power, establishing its role as the preeminent branch of the general government for the last three decades of the nineteenth century. It especially was active in accommodating corporate capitalism, even when that effort meant recasting congressional statutes through interpretation. In 1891, Congress also gave the Court the power to choose the cases it would accept, which enhanced even more the judicial role.

Political pressure for a national response to the Great Depression shifted the constitutional balance of power in economic matters to Congress and the executive, with the Court now interpreting the Constitution in ways that buttressed and extended the modern regulatory and welfare state. Congress addressed the leading issues of the day but often deferred to judges on the most hotly contested problems. In practice, this deferral resulted in a court-sanctioned, at times court-led, incremental redrawing of social and political boundaries, with claims pressed by private litigants and not, as happened in Europe, with actions undertaken by public agencies.

Significantly, the Court found encouragement for this role, as well as for its earlier protection of economic liberty, in a late-nineteenth-shift in the way Americans thought about the law. In a series of lectures in 1881, Oliver Wendell Holmes Jr., later a Supreme Court justice, argued that "the life of the law has not been logic; it has been experience." By this, he meant that social and economic change necessarily influences legal interpretation; this "legal realism," as it was called, suggested that courts were responsible for keeping law current.

Legal realism (or sociological jurisprudence) was instrumental in strengthening protection for individual rights in the twentieth century, as witnessed most recently in decisions involving rights of lesbian, gay, bisexual, and transgender individuals (LGBT). It also brought judges under attack for usurping the role of the legislature. Judicial activism was the label opponents slapped on unpopular decisions of whatever stripe, and judicial philosophy became a touchstone for supporters and opponents in Senate confirmation of federal court appointees.

Even though the Supreme Court increasingly has claimed the power to say what the Constitution means, the tug of war between Congress and the Presidency often has been more significant in developing national power than decisions from the nation's highest bench. This struggle resulted in executive power much more vigorous and legislative power both more democratic and, at times, more conservative than the framers believed they were constructing.

The Constitution defines the powers of Congress explicitly; it is much less exact in outlining presidential authority. The balance-of-powers doctrine required an executive strong enough to restrain the legislature, as well as someone to convey the strength of the nation without threatening its republican foundations. The framers made a general grant of power to the president—"The executive Power shall be vested in a President of the United States of America"—but it left unanswered what this vesting clause meant. Did it give the president inherent, unilateral authority to protect the safety and well-being of the nation? It is one of the most vexing questions of power in American constitutional history.

George Washington established the model for the office: he intuitively understood that a single national executive had two functions, administrative and ceremonial. His aim, as noted in his farewell address, was to build loyalty to the office, not the man. He embraced republican simplicity, demanded respect for the presidency, adhered scrupulously to constitutional principles, and limited his tenure to two terms, a precedent that lasted until Franklin D. Roosevelt won third and fourth terms during World War II. (The Twenty-Second Amendment, ratified in 1951 as a political reaction to Roosevelt's heresy, now limits the president to two full elected terms.) Washington acted vigorously, but he also deferred to Congress as the most representative branch of government, accepting its judgment on legislation unless he believed it clearly violated the Constitution. This precedent lasted only a generation.

The Constitution permits either an active or a passive executive. At first, the presidency largely conformed to the scheme taught in civics classes, "The President proposes and Congress disposes." Early incumbents expanded the federal bureaucracy, thereby creating a base of power, but they deferred to Congress as the law-making body. The separation and balance of powers principle suffered little, if any, erosion. It was Andrew Jackson, who served from 1829 to 1837, who claimed new powers for his office, making it recognizably modern.

Jackson added head of party to the functions of ceremonial head of state and executive head of government and used patronage to control the federal bureaucracy, which he expanded greatly. He also made political operatives key advisors (the Kitchen Cabinet) and defended his right to remove executive officers at will, even though the Senate had confirmed them. More significantly, he reshaped executive power by using the veto as a legislative weapon. Previous presidents had vetoed legislation only when they concluded that Congress had exceeded its constitutional authority. Jackson initially followed this course but when adversaries passed a bill rechartering the national bank that Jackson opposed, he vetoed it. The measure not only was unconstitutional, he argued, it was unwise.

Jackson echoed Jefferson's belief that each branch of government had an equal responsibility to judge constitutionality for itself. In combining this departmental theory of constitutional interpretation with his innovative use of the veto, Jackson inserted the executive branch into the legislative process in a way not envisioned by the framers. Congress now had to consult the president on matters before it. Today, presidents are deeply involved in the legislative process. The path to this contemporary role was not a direct one, but it began with Jackson.

Jackson's opponents complained that he had subverted the Constitution by his redefinition of presidential power, but most nineteenth-century presidents, except for Abraham Lincoln, did not follow suit, thereby failing to realize the office's potential for leadership. Many presidents served only one term, and Congress often resisted efforts to advance programs contrary to its sense of what the nation required. The establishment of a merit-based civil service in 1883, following the 1881 assassination of President James A. Garfield, also blunted the president's authority by restricting his patronage power.

The twentieth century witnessed a marked expansion of executive power and raised serious questions about whether the separation and balance doctrine was still a viable constitutional principle. The challenges to national security and economic stability placed great demands on the office, and successful presidents, notably Franklin D. Roosevelt, began to use dormant powers, such as executive orders, to achieve what were, in effect, legislative outcomes.

Congress often has been complicit in the expansion of presidential power. National emergencies of war and depression made it necessary to act swiftly and strained the capacity of Congress to respond. Beginning in the late nineteenth century Congress created administrative agencies, housed in the executive branch, with broad authority to apply its general statutes to the increasingly complex and dynamic American economy and society. The twentieth century witnessed quasi-independent federal regulatory agencies—e.g., Food and Drug Administration (FDA, 1906) and Federal Communications Commission (FCC, 1934), among a host of other alphabet agencies—to address broad national problems. The result was what some scholars have termed a fourth branch of government. This development shifted power away from Congress, a trend given impetus by the Supreme Court in 1984 with its doctrine of administrative deference (known as the Chevron deference) in which courts accept an agency's interpretation of a statute unless it is unreasonable.

The self-inflicted weakening of Congress is not a recent phenomenon. It is cyclical. Parties are an extra-constitutional development—the framers worried about such factions—but they have permitted Congress to function efficiently and with dispatch when a congressional majority and president shared a party affiliation. More often, Congress and president have been from different parties, resulting in inefficiency. A modern phenomenon, hyper-partisanship, has proved another obstacle to congressional action, even when legislative and executive branches share the same party affiliation. Although weakening Congress, both division and inaction serve as an informal set of checks and balances.

When public opinion remains unsettled—and the years since 1968 fit this description—energy has migrated to the president, with the Supreme Court providing a check on power. This circumstance, in turn, has resurrected twin concerns about power: the presidency is becoming an imperial institution, with no effective restraints, and the Supreme Court, an undemocratic institution, is making law instead of applying law. These accusations come from both sides of the political spectrum, depending on who is in office and what is at issue.

Judicial activism remains a concern, but the increase in presidential power has been more troubling. The executive branch is replete with well-staffed offices, agencies, and commissions unimaginable even in the mid-twentieth century, all justified by the demands of a complex global society. The modern president exists in splendid isolation, protected from public access except through the unrelenting focus of a 24/7 news cycle. These conditions, critics charge, have led to trappings of power that rival royalty and to presidents who consider themselves above the law. Dual claims of executive privilege and executive immunity symbolize the "imperial presidency," the first referring to the president's power to withhold information at his discretion and the second to his ability to ignore all other processes of law while in office, except for impeachment.

Courts have given wide berth to the president but in recent years have rejected both absolute privilege and absolute immunity. In *United States v. Nixon* (1974), the Court required President Nixon to turn over secretly recorded, damaging tapes for use in a criminal case in which he was an unindicted co-conspirator. Two decades later the justices rejected President Bill Clinton's claim of immunity from testimony in a civil suit unrelated to his duties, a decision that contributed to the nation's second presidential impeachment trial. These instances have been rare; traditionally, both the legislative and the judicial branch have given great deference to the executive, leading modern critics to worry that no meaningful check exists on presidential power.

Separation of powers issues are never far from the surface in modern American government. It is tempting to view the inefficiencies, tensions, and failures of a system of checks and balances as a mark of dysfunctional government. If so, it is constitutionally mandated dysfunction: "the doctrine of separation of powers was adopted not to promote efficiency," Supreme Court Justice Louis Brandeis wrote in 1926, "but to preclude the exercise of arbitrary power." The result has been both frustrating and beneficial. Checks and balances have slowed the pace of reform, yet structural restraints have permitted public opinion to develop in support of change.

The revolutionary influence on American constitutional culture remains active and vital. The United States still is a nation that fears power, especially in government, and Americans are willing to live with inefficient government because they sense that they are freer than when power faces no impediments to action. They have accepted the framers' innovative use of divided government because they too are convinced that only radical restraints on power can produce the checks on self-interest that liberty requires.

Chapter 4
Property

The Constitution gives the government power to protect and promote the nation's economic interests. It would have been unthinkable in 1787 to do otherwise. The unfettered ability to acquire and own property was chief among those interests. The revolutionaries believed that the right to property was a natural law: it ensured freedom by providing self-sufficiency, the condition that allowed men to resist arbitrary government. "Property must be secured," John Adams wrote, "or liberty cannot exist."

The Constitution of 1787 contains no broad guarantee of the right to property, but it established numerous protections for property, many of which had analogues in the various state constitutions. It shielded landed wealth from federal taxation by forbidding a direct tax unless apportioned by population. Other clauses forbade export duties, bills of attainder, and forfeiture of property upon conviction for a crime. The Constitution also granted broad powers of taxation and authority to regulate interstate and foreign commerce. Congress could establish uniform laws of bankruptcy and grant patents and copyrights. The states could not tax imports and exports nor pass any law "impairing the obligation of contracts." Finally, the framers protected property in slaves: Congress could not prohibit the slave trade until 1808; fugitive slaves had to be surrendered upon claim; and three-fifths of a state's slave population would count for purposes of representation and taxation, which boosted the clout of slave-holding states.

The right to property found explicit protection in the Constitution with adoption of the Fifth Amendment in 1791. It embraced the Lockean idea that protection of property was a central aim of government: "No person shall be deprived of life, liberty, or property, without due process of law; nor shall private property be taken for public use, without just compensation." Many terms were ambiguous—What was property? Due process? Public use? Just compensation?—but James Madison believed they should be construed broadly. The aim, he argued, was to protect people's right to the free use of their property.

Many modern commentators portray the framers as capitalists, imbued with the free-market theories of Adam Smith, whose masterwork, *The Wealth of Nations*, appeared in 1776. It is an attractive but inaccurate conceit. The Constitution is agnostic on matters of economic theory; the men who wrote it were not. They were not capitalists as we understand the term, which did not come into common use until the nineteenth century. Rather, they were commercially minded republicans who assumed that government's role was to foster and manage an economy to ensure a favorable balance of trade.

The framers' commercial republicanism placed a different emphasis on the economic role of government than the neutrality Adam Smith advocated. Alexander Hamilton's plans to use governmental power as an economic engine embodied these ideas. For Hamilton and his followers, the Constitution empowered government to protect property and secure contractual rights that, in turn, made it possible for ambitious men to create wealth, which, in their view, was compatible with republican virtues. Government had an obligation to trigger economic growth, using its considerable power to develop a national market and stimulate investment in the capital-scarce young republic.

Capitalism ultimately proved suitable to the American circumstances of cheap, abundant land, widespread ownership of property, and a desire to maximize liberty by restraining governmental power, but it is misleading to read the Constitution as an endorsement of this economic theory. More significant is how courts and judges reshaped the law of property as a capitalist instrument in ways that fit both constitutional republicanism and an emerging democratic order. By the 1830s Americans and their lawmakers increasingly read the Constitution as a brief for an entrepreneurial free market.

How to divide competing powers over the economy between state and central governments, especially in matters of contract and commerce, became an important issue in the new nation. The Marshall Court spent much of its energy drawing these lines. Early on, federal judges used the extra-constitutional doctrine of vested rights to protect existing economic relationships. Under this Lockean notion, mentioned nowhere in the Constitution, the right to property was guaranteed by natural law. Any law that disturbed property rights was unconstitutional because it violated one of the general principles limiting all governments. The Marshall Court linked this doctrine to the contract clause and used it to promote a national economy, a goal that required strengthening national government and limiting state power.

An initial step extended constitutional protection to contracts made by states as well as by private citizens. In 1796, the state of Georgia reneged on a large land-grant linked to bribery. Marshall declared the repeal an unconstitutional violation of the contract clause when the case reached the court in 1810. The contract clause, he wrote, embraced "the general principles, which are common to our free institutions," a phrase that tied vested rights to the Constitution.

Later decisions extended the contract clause to other state economic actions: a tax exemption that New Jersey granted to a band of American Indians was a non-violable contract; a corporate charter was a constitutionally protected contract (*Dartmouth College v. Woodward*, 1819); a bankruptcy law could not retroactively discharge contractual obligations. The *Dartmouth College* case was noteworthy because it offered constitutional protection to the corporation, a form of enterprise traditionally used by charitable and public functions but increasingly adopted by businesses as a way of limiting risk.

Increasingly Americans believed in the power of the free market to allocate resources, enhance wealth, and provide economic opportunities. This notion of an unfettered market open to all had its political equivalent in democratic individualism, and both strands of this new American ethic influenced key constitutional themes. For democracy, the demand for universal white adult male suffrage required a recasting of the representative principle; for capitalism, the free market demanded the sanctity of contracts as a barrier against government interference with private economic arrangements. It was not an accidental marriage. Both ideas reflected the triumph of individualism and free will as primary values that Americans expected the Constitution to protect.

The mid-nineteenth century witnessed a reinterpretation of the contract clause. A Court with different membership and a new leader, Roger B. Taney (1836–1864), a Jacksonian disciple, served during a time when the nation's dramatic transformation was evident even to the most casual observer. Rapid advances in transportation facilitated demographic and economic growth by opening the interior to settlement, with cities as regional trade centers. The corporation began to replace traditional partnerships and single-owner businesses, setting the stage for the accumulation of capital and economies of scale that made later industrialization possible. It was in this environment that Taney sought to reconcile the interpretations of his predecessor with the new realities of American life.

A classic case, *Charles River Bridge v. Warren Bridge* (1837), gave the Taney Court an opportunity to make this accommodation of old and new. In 1785, Massachusetts chartered the Charles River Bridge Company to build a bridge connecting Boston and Charlestown, with a right to collect tolls for forty years (later extended to seventy years). Within a few years traffic increased, and the state granted the Warren Bridge Company the right to build a nearby bridge that would become state property after six years. The Charles River Bridge Company claimed that its charter, a contract, implied an exclusive right to collect tolls; otherwise, investors would not have risked their money.

Charles River Bridge v. Warren Bridge brought together questions of great importance to the future of constitutional law: What was the status of corporations? What effect would new technologies have on existing agreements? How much control over the economy could states exercise? But it was the reshaping of the contracts clause that tied the nation's constitutional past to its capitalist future. Taney did not repudiate the *Dartmouth College* decision that the state could not impair a charter, but he refused to interpret the contract to include any implied right. The real issue was progress: would existing contracts be allowed to hinder economic growth? The question was not hypothetical. Railroads already were speeding the flow of goods to market, and a decision for the Charles River Bridge Company would only blunt their development.

Taney understood that abandonment of the old to make way for the new—what the later economic scholar Joseph Schumpeter called the process of "creative destruction"—is integral to capitalism. The *Charles River Bridge* case was an exemplar of a major transformation of American law that sacrificed concepts of vested rights and natural law to the demands of progress. It did not undermine the right to property but made clear that the nation's economic future demanded dynamic, not static, forms of property.

As states found new ways to promote economic growth, the Taney Court sought to balance legislative authority with the right of contract. The justices ruled that legislatures could not modify the terms of contract to favor debtors, but they also ruled that eminent domain did not violate the contract clause even when it destroyed the value of a franchise. This latter decision left states free to experiment with their power to take property for public use, often to the detriment of property rights. The Court also gave wide latitude to states in the exercise of police powers, although not always to promote economic development The majority of justices were state-sovereignty Southerners who shied from any ruling that implied a national power to restrict this most politically volatile class of property.

Unrestrained property ownership enjoyed widespread support, and judges assumed a more active role as special guardians of property rights, a stance with major implications for the coming industrial age. Symbolic of their new claim, the Supreme Court ruled that a general judge-made commercial law of the United States existed, even though no constitutional provision or congressional statute established it. Under this standard, federal judges would become the touchstone for economic decisions, including the right to property, which increasingly they decided was paramount to the protection of the public welfare. The laissez-faire jurisprudence of the late nineteenth century stemmed directly from the property-conscious law of antebellum America.

From 1865 to 1900 the United States experienced dramatic economic transformations. Work was mechanized, both in manufacturing and in agriculture; national markets emerged in food, clothing, and durable goods, with economies of scale reducing costs to consumers but often harming local suppliers and businessmen; and standards of living improved, especially for a rapidly growing urban middle class. These transitions were not smooth or uniform in their effect: the economy experienced steep depressions in 1873 and 1893; labor often clashed violently with owners over pay, hours, and working conditions; urban poverty and crime were major problems; politics was unusually partisan; and government at all levels was overwhelmed, unstable, and often corrupt.

The late nineteenth century also was a time of a momentous legal transformation, with rights of property at the center of a new constitutionalism based on free-market capitalism. The challenge was how to reconcile a legal framework built for a highly decentralized agrarian society, with its emphasis on restraint of public power, to the needs of an urban, industrial nation in which private or corporate power came to be seen not only as an engine of prosperity but also as a threat to liberty.

From the time of Marshall, American judges had sought to make law a science based on reason. Under this framework, jurists believed that law had two branches—public law and private law. Public law embraced the actions of government and ultimately was political. It responded to the popular will and, in economic matters, its tendency was to regulate and redistribute wealth. Private law, such as the law of property and contracts, protected the exercise of individual will and was essential to the functioning of a free market. Only judges, in this view, could serve as neutral arbiters between the conflicting demands of public and private law.

The distinction between public and private law was a fiction—in a democracy, law always is political—but it expressed a powerful Anglo-American ethical tradition that government should not advance the interest of one party over another. The attacks on vested rights, monopolies, and special interests from Jefferson through Jackson and beyond were part of this legacy that promoted individual liberty as its highest goal. Any governmental restraints on this liberty were suspect.

This view achieved ascendancy on the Court in the late nineteenth century, beginning with two dissents in the *Slaughterhouse Cases* in 1873. The majority justices rejected the claim of New Orleans butchers that the privileges and immunities and due process clauses of the Fourteenth Amendment protected their right to process their cattle outside of a state-chartered slaughterhouse. But dissenting justices fashioned a doctrine known later as economic due process, which soon became a majority position. The issue was not whether the legal process was fair but whether it was reasonable and produced a fair result; judges would decide if it adhered to free-market principles, not legislators beholden to special interests. This approach was a clear expression of laissez-faire constitutionalism: economic liberty and personal liberty were the same, and the right to own and use property unimpeded by government became a judicial touchstone of American freedom.

Economic due process (also known as substantive due process) replaced the contract clause as the most important constitutional doctrine protecting property rights. With reasonableness now a judicial question, the Supreme Court in 1898 abandoned a two-decades-old standard allowing states to regulate railroad prices and established a formula to guarantee a fair return to utilities. Combined with an earlier decision that corporations were legal persons protected by due process, the Court became the overseer of state economic regulation. The effect was to make the judiciary the arbiter of interstate commerce.

By the end of the nineteenth century, the Court announced a newly discovered and widely accepted liberty of contract: individuals owned their skills and talents, with no debt to society, and parties to a bargain entered it freely and on equal terms. The unfettered marketplace became a metaphor for liberty itself. Even exploited groups defined their aspirations in market terms, for example, women's equality depended on an ability to control property independently of men.

Elsewhere, the Court interpreted expansively the takings and just compensation requirements of the Fifth Amendment.

In 1897, it unanimously decided that the Fourteenth Amendment incorporated the just compensation clause of the Fifth Amendment, making it the first use of the Bill of Rights to restrain state action (*Chicago, Burlington and Quincy Railroad Company v. Chicago*). The Court restricted state power to regulate railroads and interstate trade yet also limited federal authority to intercede in the market by denying the Interstate Commerce Commission, the nation's first administrative agency, the power to set railroad rates. It also defined commerce as trade and transportation only, not production (specifically not manufacturing), thereby limiting congressional authority and preserving the traditional state power to regulate business, even though it was apparent that many state legislatures were prisoners of corporate interests. Finally, the justices interpreted the federal power to tax narrowly, ruling that an 1894 federal income tax was unconstitutional.

It is easy to criticize the Court's embrace of economic due process and its exaltation of laissez-faire capitalism, but the justices were responding to significant problems not addressed elsewhere. The patchwork of state regulations imposed a burden on corporations that operated in a national market. By imposing standards on the rate-fixing process, the Court protected the accumulation of investment capital. It also sought to remove obstacles to interstate trade. But the justices were less involved in establishing a new constitutional framework than in reifying an older one. Theirs was a nineteenth-century jurisprudence that made the rights of property and economic liberty a primary object for governmental protection. Economic theory had become an article of constitutional faith.

Progressives and other reformers assailed the notion that courts, not elected legislatures, were the proper forum for resolving property and contract disputes. They attacked the notion that the Constitution enshrined laissez-faire economic theory. Reformers perceived threats to democracy in the growing gap between rich and poor, the economic distress of farmers and urban laborers, the corrupting influence of money in politics, and, above all, the concentration and abuse of private power. Private power, represented by corporate capitalism, was a danger to liberty, posing the same threat as an overweening government.

The reformers' remedy was the regulatory state, in which administrative agencies staffed by experts with technical skills corrected the imbalance of power in the new industrial order. One goal was to preserve competition in the face of corporate monopolies; another was to alleviate the harshness of industrial employment and urban life. States were laboratories for experimentation, with measures such as workmen's compensation, minimum-wage and maximum-hour rules for workers, and health and safety standards infringing the right to property and the liberty of contract as expressed in laissez-faire constitutionalism. Reformers argued that law must be judged by its results. Emblematic of this new stance was the "Brandeis brief," a tactic made popular by the progressive lawyer (and later Supreme Court Justice) Louis D. Brandeis, who larded his pleadings with non-legal evidence on the social and economic effects of laws and decisions that he sought to reverse.

The justification for this new regulatory posture could be found in state police power, which progressives interpreted broadly but which flew in the teeth of economic due process. Laissez-faire constitutionalism reached its zenith in *Lochner v. New York* (1905), when the Court, by a vote of 5-4, struck down a state law that restricted work in bakeries to ten hours a day and sixty hours a week. The majority opinion not only disagreed with the legislative judgment that baking was unhealthy, it also doubted the legislature's honesty. The real reason for the law, it concluded, was to regulate labor relations, which violated the constitutionally protected liberty of contract.

The election of progressives to national and state offices— Presidents Theodore Roosevelt and Woodrow Wilson were both

3. Nearly a year after entering World War I, the US government nationalized the railroads in order to meet wartime economic needs. In 1920, following much debate, a railroad bill denationalizing ownership moved through both houses of Congress and to President Woodrow Wilson's desk. Clifford Berryman's caricature demonstrates the separation of powers specified by the Constitution.

reformers—led to an assault on the old order. Regulatory agencies and commissions such as the Food and Drug Administration and the Federal Reserve Board, effectively a fourth branch of government, embraced governmental power to restrict property rights and restrain the excesses of corporate capitalism.

Reform also came to the Constitution itself. Twice, Congress passed and states ratified amendments that redefined property rights. The Sixteenth Amendment (1913) enabled Congress to tax incomes, which funded the regulatory state and lessened the laissez-faire protection of property by taxing wealth.

The Eighteenth Amendment (1919) was a more direct assault on property rights by halting the manufacture and sale of intoxicating liquors, effectively destroying its value. A third amendment, the Seventeenth (1913), made senators popularly elected—previously, state legislatures made the selection—which eliminated a corrupt mode of election too often controlled by corporate interests.

The New Deal (1933–40) marked the end of laissez-faire constitutionalism. Faced with unemployment of 25 percent, unprecedented corporate failures, and a bankrupt financial system, President Franklin D. Roosevelt rejected free-market solutions—market failure led to the problems, he concluded—and embraced unprecedented government intervention in the economy. During the new administration's first one hundred days, Congress used its ommerce-clause power to regulate the stock market, set wages and prices, create a government-owned energy producer (the Tennessee Valley Authority, or TVA), and provide poof relief. Later laws established Social Security and new regulatory agencies.

The New Deal was frankly experimental, and its programs failed as often as they succeeded. It did not end the Great Depression, although its approach of massive fiscal stimulus did. World War II spending—and the enlistment of millions of men into the armed services—ultimately solved the widespread under-consumption and unemployment that prolonged the Depression. Even so, the New Deal's constitutional importance cannot be overstated. It used governmental power to control private excess in pursuit of public liberty and warred with the rigid notions of limited government, marketplace competition, and sanctity of property rights that marked the constitutional order.

New Dealers feared that the Supreme Court would block their reforms, and the justices did not disappoint their expectations. The confrontation came first in 1935 when the Court struck down four New Deal measures that regulated various industries. The justices upheld only the TVA (as a national defense measure). Never had the Court overturned so many acts of Congress in such a short period of time.

A political backlash against these decisions produced a constitutional crisis. In 1937, a newly reelected president Roosevelt unveiled a plan to restructure the Court, an action permitted to Congress by Article III of the Constitution. Lack of popular support forced Roosevelt to drop the plan, but the justices had read the election returns, and they soon upheld a series of New Deal measures. The repudiation of the old order was clear when the Court upheld a state minimum wage law, noting explicitly that "the Constitution does not speak of liberty of contract." The right of property was not immune from regulation by a democratic majority or the bureaucracy that acted on its behalf.

The degree of judicial oversight also changed. In a now-famous "Footnote Four," Justice Harlan Fiske Stone introduced the idea of levels of judicial scrutiny (*United States v. Carolene Products Co.*, 1938). When a law or action, on its face, is within a constitutionally authorized power, the Court would assume its reasonableness and apply minimal oversight—but not when a law falls within an area strictly prohibited by the Constitution, as was the case with the Bill of Rights. The shift could not have been more dramatic, as was clear two decades later when Justice Hugo Black, writing for the majority in 1963, said, "We refuse to sit as a 'super legislature'... [W]hether the legislature takes as its textbook Adam Smith, Herbert Spencer, or Lord Keynes or some other is no concern of ours."

The constitutional double standard proposed by Footnote Four quickly became the new orthodoxy. Since the constitutional revolution of 1937, Congress has had free rein in matters of economic policy under an expansive interpretation of the commerce clause. The Court repeatedly has limited the states' ability to isolate or protect their businesses or citizens from national regulations, for example, by striking down a state's prohibition of imported waste materials or giving its residents preferred access to natural resources.

The Court's retreat on economic matters opened the door to the modern regulatory state. Footnote Four's distinction between property rights and personal liberty would have confounded the framers, who thought of the Constitution as a check on threats to property posed by a democratic majority. Critics have noted the anomaly of imagining that the Fifth Amendment protected liberty more than property, but the Court has denied that it thinks of the two as separate: "A fundamental interdependence exists between the personal right to liberty and the personal right to property," the justices proclaimed in 1972. "Neither could have meaning without the other."

In recent decades, a conservative attack on this New Deal constitutionalism has emerged among scholars who have asserted the superiority of a private market and seek to apply a cost-benefit analysis to public regulation. This philosophy had appeal in a political environment that, by the end of the 1960s, had grown weary of reform and regulation. Republican victories in all but three presidential elections from 1968 to 2016 produced lower federal court judges who were sympathetic to this view, as well as to a jurisprudence based on originalism as the only legitimate basis for constitutional interpretation. But the deep recession of 2008–10, and especially the need for governments around the world to intervene vigorously in financial markets, called into question the assumption of a rational, beneficent market and in the desirability of an unregulated or lightly monitored economy. Once again Americans were reminded that unbridled private power was as much a threat to liberty as unlimited governmental power.

The United States, indeed the world, has changed radically since the Revolution—then, only 3 percent of the nation was urban;

today, eight of ten residents live in a city; then, markets were limited, local, and isolated; today, they are boundless, linked, and international—but the fundamental questions about the role of government remain. What has become apparent over two centuries of constitutional jurisprudence, however, is how often private ownership is in tension with popular sovereignty, democracy, and the general welfare. How to strike an appropriate balance between these legitimate constitutional interests remains a challenge, one that contemporary Americans share with the founding generation, who viewed this tension as a mainspring of liberty.

Chapter 5
Representation

More than most constitutional issues, questions of representation and suffrage have exposed the fault lines of class, race, and gender in American society. Popular sovereignty was the touchstone of republican liberty, but only grudgingly did rulers admit the ruled into their circle. The worldview of the framers had no room for women, blacks, Indians, or the poor as citizens worthy of the ballot. It took a series of constitutional amendments, all spurred by war or mass movements, to expand the electorate and redefine "we the people" to include all adult citizens as rulers.

Western societies traditionally viewed hierarchical authority as natural, but revolutionary republicanism embraced a different premise: the people could rule themselves. Representation was the means to express consent, but the American experience required that the connection between the representative and the represented be direct, or local. (Great Britain practiced virtual representation whereby members of Parliament represented all Englishmen everywhere.) Without the bonds of shared geography and mutual interests, the people could not give consent; without the people's consent, no legitimate representation existed. After independence, this formula of popular consent and representation became the measure for republican government.

Popular sovereignty had radical implications for government because it made democracy part of the new Constitution. At first, it was a nebulous link. With the popular unrest of the 1780s fresh in their minds, the framers sought to restrain and guide democracy. The Constitution contains no right to vote, although it guarantees to each state a republican form of government, an implicit recognition of the right, and specifies the nature of the electorate for the House of Representatives. Elsewhere, the institutions of government relied upon a careful architecture to ensure that the will of the people could emerge deliberately rather than as an unrestrained impulse.

But who were the people? The Constitution not only failed to define national citizenship, it left the question of who could vote to the discretion of the states. Few delegates supported an expanded vote, much less universal suffrage. Practical considerations were at play. State constitutions already established qualifications for citizenship and voting, and they differed significantly. An attempt to define these terms could jeopardize ratification, especially because slavery complicated the question of citizenship. Most states agreed, however, that only men of property could cast a ballot.

Property qualifications for voting had a long history. Colonists had adopted the English practice that required a man to own property taxed at forty shillings to be eligible to vote. In England, few adult males owned property worth this much tax. America was different; abundant, cheap land meant that most adult males qualified to vote. The knowledge that so many men could participate in government outweighed concern about the ones who could not. These voters were responsible for ensuring fidelity to liberty—and a duty to elect (and defer to) wise leaders.

But the idea of the people as rulers carried an internal dynamic that set it at odds with beliefs about the virtues of deference. The Revolution unleashed a democratic spirit—the later French visitor

Alexis de Tocqueville termed it a "habit of the heart"—based on equality combined with the civic obligations of republicanism. All men had a duty to participate in government. Americans took this obligation seriously.

Suffrage was the means of ensuring representative and responsive government. Two waves of state constitution-making, the first in the 1820s and the second in the 1850s, led to the abolition of property requirements, resulting in nearly universal white adult male suffrage. Even aliens (foreigners) could vote in most states outside the Northeast, on the belief that it would induce them to settle. The United States was not alone in this democratic impulse—western Europe too experienced it—but nowhere was the right to vote more broadly defined than in America.

It is tempting to attribute this development to an unalloyed desire to expand democracy. The idea was powerful but more was at work. The growth of urban areas meant that fewer men met property qualifications, which meant fewer men eligible to serve on juries or in the militia. A limited electorate also raised questions about the legitimacy of government, the exercise of power, and even what it meant to be free. Partisan politics played a role as well. Federalists and Republicans and then Democrats and Whigs vigorously sought voters who shared their respective visions for society.

Few advocates of a broadened franchise thought they were extending it to the lower classes, immigrants, and former farm laborers who worked for wages in the nation's new factories. Rhode Island offers a case in point. Its textile mills and small manufacturing attracted thousands of immigrants to Providence and other urban areas. The landowner-dominated legislature rejected a new state constitution in 1841 that included universal male suffrage, in large measure because of nativist concerns. What followed was an armed march on the capital and the subsequent

4. George Caleb Bingham's *The County Election* (1852) depicts the polling place at the county seat where, over a few days, farmers would vote—though not in secret. The words on the banner, a variation of the Missouri motto, read, "The will of the people, the supreme law," suggesting faith in the democratic process.

arrest of protest organizers. In an 1849 case stemming from Dorr's Rebellion (named after its leader), the US Supreme Court declined to interpret the Constitution's guarantee of "a republican form of government" to require states to be democratic or more completely representative.

Dorr's Rebellion was a harbinger of class-based efforts in the late nineteenth century to restrict the vote as waves of eastern and southern Europeans, Jews, and Asians flooded the nation's cities. But it was an outlier during the pre–Civil War decades. Democracy, with its emphasis on popular consent, was the new American gospel. It roiled the nation with its promise of individual equality in a more perfect union: "The country is full of rebellion; the country is full of kings," essayist Ralph Waldo Emerson observed in the mid-1840s. Participation in the nation's affairs did not apply to women, blacks, and certain categories of white men, most often paupers, migrants, and felons, but few people doubted that the United States had birthed a new democratic age.

The Civil War and Reconstruction embedded representative democracy as the mode of constitutional government in the United States. Modern warfare has a leveling influence—the battlefield does not honor class distinctions—and the emphasis on equality and democracy as core constitutional values stemmed in part from its effects. The Reconstruction amendments made this clear by advancing a new, inclusive definition of citizenship depending solely on place of birth (or naturalization). They also pledged national power to ensure equal protection of law for all citizens and introduced a new equation that linked liberty, equality, and democracy. Freedom for all people (Thirteenth), unconditional equality before the law for all citizens (Fourteenth), and guaranteed access to the ballot box (Fifteenth) provided the constitutional frame for this turn.

From Reconstruction to 1920, two stories of democratic constitutionalism emerged. One was its formal expansion to excluded groups, as expressed through the right to vote; the more disturbing story was restriction of the right in law and practice. In 1876, the Supreme Court held that the Fifteenth Amendment did not confer the right to vote but only prohibited exclusion on racial grounds; it also eviscerated key provisions of the law passed to enforce the amendment. Throughout the South blacks effectively lost the right to vote by literacy tests, grandfather clauses, poll taxes, and intimidation because it was easy to deny the vote by legitimate means. As one black Georgia voter poignantly testified before a Senate committee, "You may vote till your eyes drop out...[but] there's a hole in the bottom of the boxes some way and lets out our vote."

A desire to limit voting by class also was common, as witnessed by an Alabama leader's promise to keep "ignorant, incompetent, and vicious" white men from the polling booth. The effort worked. In Mississippi, for instance, turnout plummeted from 70 percent in the 1870s to 15 percent in the early twentieth century, a level that suggests how severely the new restrictions curbed not only black but also poor white voting.

The issue in the North centered on the 25 million new immigrants who flooded its cities from 1870 to 1920. Most arrivals were poor laborers—"dangerous classes"—from southern and eastern Europe who supported big-city political machines. Middle-class reformers sought to lessen their electoral influence by repudiating the notion that voting was a right and pushing for restrictions to purify the electorate. Literacy requirements (use of the Australian or secret ballot, a widely adopted reform, meant that voters must be able to read), exclusion of paupers, residency requirements, and elimination of alien suffrage were common. The Constitution posed no barrier because the Supreme Court interpreted the Reconstruction amendments to bar only official, overt discrimination. In practice, states had a free hand in determining who could vote and how.

The campaign for woman's suffrage offered both a confirmation and a counterpoint to efforts to restrict the vote for other Americans. The Fourteenth and the Fifteenth Amendments specifically guaranteed the vote in federal elections to male citizens over 21 (Fourteenth) and by barring abridgement of suffrage based on "race, color, or pervious condition of servitude," a standard that excluded white women. Woman suffrage implied an equality that went against cultural assumptions and held the unwelcome potential for wholesale restructuring of domestic and property law.

The US Supreme Court was no friendlier to women than drafters of the Reconstruction amendments had been. The justices shared the cultural assumptions of the age. In 1875, they ruled unanimously that the Fourteenth Amendment did not prevent states from confining the right to vote to men alone. Two years earlier they decided that it did not protect a woman's petition for membership in the Illinois bar, with a concurring opinion noting, "[T]he natural and proper timidity and delicacy which belongs to the female sex evidently unfits it for many of the occupations of civil life."

Blocked by the Court and by an equally resistant Congress, woman suffragists adopted a state-by-state strategy. The territory of Wyoming granted women the vote in 1869, and reaffirmed it upon statehood in 1889. By the mid-1890s three other western states—Utah, Colorado, and Idaho—had enfranchised women. Elsewhere, women made small gains in state and local elections, such as municipal and school offices, that were not governed by constitutional restrictions. To gain traction, advocates for woman suffrage argued that white, middle-class women outnumbered immigrants, blacks, and paupers and would counterbalance the ballots of these less desirable groups. This antidemocratic claim had little success. Among suffragists, the period from 1896 to 1910 became known as "the doldrums" because it produced so few victories.

Reform had rested too much on the energies of activists, many of whom did not represent the interests of either elite or working women. Once the movement became more diverse and better organized, it built an irresistible momentum for constitutional change. One key to its success was an ideological shift from xenophobia and class politics to social reform. Suffragists tied their cause to wider Progressive Era concerns about economic power and exploitation of workers and promoted the vote as a protection for working women.

The engagement of working-class women brought new support from trade unions and socialist groups. This coalition began to

5. The first woman suffrage organization in Tennessee was founded in Memphis in 1889, and many similar groups followed over the next three decades. Not only did they organize rallies and business meetings and distribute literature, but they also hosted social events such as a barbecue featuring a race between an automobile with a female driver and an airplane with a female pilot.

earn victories, with eight states granting women the vote by 1913. Two year later the various national woman suffrage organizations settled on a strategy of amending the Constitution. World War I became a catalyst for victory; entry into the conflict, justified as a democratic crusade, spurred a demand to extend the vote to women. Congress quickly passed a constitutional amendment and submitted it for ratification. In August 1920, the Nineteenth Amendment became part of the Constitution.

War once again was important in crystallizing support for a more democratic Constitution. Both the Fifteenth Amendment and the Nineteenth Amendment—and, later, the Twenty-Sixth Amendment (1971) lowering the voting age to 18—followed conflicts in which excluded groups made important contributions to the war effort. In a limited sense, these amendments were products of the moment. But they also had a long gestation. Democratic constitutionalism was more than an impulse; it was the result of social, economic, and political changes that persuaded the nation to redefine its fundamental law. Formal access to the ballot box, however, did not remove the obstacles to political participation for either blacks or women. Southern white opposition and northern indifference left African Americans politically marginalized, a circumstance that did not change until the civil rights movement of the 1950s and 1960s. For women, gender bias hindered their entry into politics, and they too had to wait decades before reaping the fruits of their democratic labors.

Constitutional democracy scored another success in the Progressive Era with the ratification in 1913 of the Seventeenth Amendment requiring the popular election of US senators. Election by state legislatures had become marked by corruption and political chaos. Rejecting the debased system, twenty-nine states adopted direct election, and after the fraudulent election of an Illinois senator in 1911, a recalcitrant US Senate finally supported the measure. The amendment was part of a package of reforms designed to cure the ills of democracy by creating more democracy. State-controlled direct primary elections, restrictions on campaign contributions and lobbying activities, and initiative and referendum were intended to circumvent state legislatures and allow voters to pass state laws directly. Recall of elected officials also was part of the prescription for reform. These changes usually were aimed at state and local governments, although some had counterparts in federal law (such as limits on lobbying and campaign contributions), and they reflected a desire to keep government close to the people.

Another amendment, also part of the progressive agenda, made it possible for the national government to become an engine of national reform. The Sixteenth Amendment, ratified in 1913, legitimized a federal income tax, which the Supreme Court had declared unconstitutional in 1895 despite its use during the Civil War. Although its impact was not immediate, the income tax gave the central government the financial means to respond vigorously to important national problems, including demands for an energetic democratic constitutionalism that arose again after World War II.

Democratic revisions of the Constitution did not end in 1920. The Twenty-Third (1961), Twenty-Fourth (1964), and Twenty-Sixth (1971) Amendments all advanced this aim. The Twenty-Third Amendment forbade states from levying a poll tax; the Twenty-Fourth granted residents of the District of Columbia the right to vote for electors in presidential contests; and the Twenty-Sixth guaranteed eighteen-year-olds the right to vote. These amendments were a clear public commitment to universal suffrage, which now was central to representation.

Other amendments aimed to increase the national government's responsiveness to popular rule. Shifting the start of a new presidential term from March 4 to January 20 (Twentieth Amendment, 1933), prompted by the emergency of the Great Depression, was an effort to vest authority and accountability more quickly in the people's choice. Limiting the president and vice president to two terms (Twenty-Second, 1951), a Republican-led reaction to Franklin D. Roosevelt's four consecutive electoral victories, mandated a turnover in office that recalled Andrew Jackson's call for democratic rotation.

The voting amendments embraced democracy as a core value, but they were not self-enforcing. Throughout the last half of the nineteenth century and well into the twentieth, neither Congress nor the Supreme Court actively pursued remedies when state actions blocked black access to the ballot box. By the mid-twentieth century, however, the success of the civil rights movement persuaded both legislators and justices to make democratic values part of statutory and constitutional law. In 1953, the Court finally outlawed the southern white primary, concluding a three-decade long series of cases that whittled away at its exclusion of black voters. Soon a more liberal Court, led by Chief Justice Earl Warren, increasingly interpreted the Fourteenth Amendment's due process and equal protection clauses as outlawing practices that violated fairness and representative self-government.

A radical break with precedent came in the early 1960s when the Court turned to legislative redistricting. When the Tennessee legislature in 1962 failed to reapportion every decade as required by the state constitution—a failure that effectively disenfranchised urban voters—the majority justices warned that failure to do so would violate the Fourteenth Amendment's equal protection clause. Two years later, in *Reynolds v. Sims* (1964), the Court settled on the standard of "one person, one vote" to govern these politically volatile questions. The Constitution required that each person's vote count the same, or as Warren wrote for the Court: "Legislatures represent people, not trees or acres." The decision has wide-ranging impact. At least one house in nearly all the states and both houses in most were unrepresentative. Soon the principle of equal representation extended to the local level. These cases reaffirmed that "fair and effective representation for all citizens," as Warren asserted in *Reynolds*, was a central tenet of democratic constitutionalism.

What this principle meant in practice was a more vexing question, especially because *Reynolds* also had spoken of unconstitutional arrangements that diluted the weight of a person's vote, as, for example, when legislators drew equal but intentionally white-majority districts. The Voting Rights Act of 1965 anticipated some of these issues. It mandated national supervision of voting, especially in southern states where hostile legislatures and unsympathetic federal judges had barred African Americans from the polls. Not only could federal marshals be used to ensure

The U.S. Constitution

minority suffrage, but states with a history of discrimination had to obtain preclearance from the Justice Department for any changes in their election laws.

Challenged by the affected states, the Supreme Court affirmed the measure in 1966 as a valid exercise of power under the Fifteenth Amendment's enforcement clause. It also invoked the equal protection clause of the Fourteenth Amendment by upholding the provision that banned New York from using English-only ballots to exclude the large number of Spanish-speaking Puerto Ricans in New York City. The Court's decisions clearly affirmed two basic precepts: all racial barriers to voting were illegal, and the national government had the power to ensure race-neutral elections.

The Voting Rights Act also attacked wealth as a barrier to voting by instructing the attorney general to seek a test of the constitutionality of state poll taxes, which resulted in a 1966 Supreme Court decision forbidding the practice. (The Twenty-Third Amendment banned poll taxes only in federal elections.) For the first time in the nation's history, a majority of justices rejected all economic restrictions on voting. Three years later the Court adopted a "strict scrutiny" standard for evaluating the constitutionality of voting statutes because these laws "constitute the foundation of our representative society." Over the course of a decade, both the Court and Congress had linked the Fourteenth Amendment's equal protection clause to the Fifteenth Amendment and extended it to other forms of voting discrimination not expressly forbidden by the Constitution.

Broadened several times to include Latinos, Asian Americans, and American Indians, most recently in 2006, the Voting Rights Act resulted in substantial increases in both minority voters and officeholders. It also raised an important new question about the meaning of representation and constitutional democracy. Were minorities as groups entitled to a proportionate number of representatives or, at a minimum, to districts in which they were

71

the majority? The question was not abstract because legislators still had legitimate means to dilute the impact of minority votes, for example, through creation of multimember districts.

Americans were too individualistic to accept the idea that representation could be tied to racially defined groups. Consistent with this belief, the Supreme Court in 1993 held that racial gerrymandering, that is, ensuring a majority for any racial group, normally would not be constitutional. The vote was an individual right that belonged to all adult citizens equally. The true constitutional measure was whether each vote was meaningful. By the twenty-first century, with numerous examples of black candidates elected by majority white electorates, including the first African American president, many people found it difficult to argue otherwise.

By the early 1970s, with the right to vote nationalized, the United States had near universal suffrage as a matter of constitutional law. Wealth, race, gender, and literacy, among other characteristics, no longer disqualified adults from voting. The Voting Rights Act nationalized voting standards, and in 1993 the National Voter Registration Act, also known as the Motor Voter Law, required states to enlist voters when they visited local motor vehicle bureaus or applied for social services. The act was the final step in removing impediments to voting and meet the demands of democratic constitutionalism. Under it, registrations increased dramatically, disproportionately drawn from the young, black, and high-school educated who tended to vote Democratic, the result feared by Republicans who had opposed the bill.

Critics of the measure began to charge that easy access was a cover for voter fraud across the nation. Even though registrations grew, turnout did not increase, in part because new restrictions appeared in many states requiring official identification to receive a ballot. In 2008, a conservative but sharply divided Supreme

Court upheld a strict Indiana law against what the legislature deemed to be the risk of voter fraud, even though the state offered no evidence that it was a problem.

The next decade witnessed a host of new laws to tighten access to the ballot box, especially in states controlled by Republicans who were concerned about the effect of unfavorable demographic trends on their electoral prospects. Even with the new demands for stringency, the historically long list of restrictions on voting had dwindled to only a few, good behavior chief among them. The largest disenfranchised group was ex-felons, mostly African American and Latino men, estimated at more than four million in 2010. Many recent state and national restoration efforts have sought to end this last major impediment to voting, even though it has been deemed constitutional by the Supreme Court.

Other problems remained with the voting process. A sharply divided Court halted the bitterly contested recount in the presidential election of 2000 because the majority held that the lack of uniformity in how to count votes violated the equal protection clause, but the decision affected only Florida (*Bush v. Gore*, 2000). More recently, in 2013, the justices by a narrow margin invalidated the preclearance provisions of the Voting Rights Act, which led to efforts to tighten voting requirements in most of the previously affected states. These problems were not insignificant but they did not change the result of several decades of reform: after two centuries, voting was clearly established as a right of all adult citizens in the nation's fundamental law as well as in public opinion.

Of course, the story of constitutional democracy does not end with universal suffrage. Class, wealth, gender, and race no longer are qualifications for suffrage but they are not inconsequential in shaping what representation means in fact. The power of money is evident in every presidential election and increasingly in state and local elections. Campaign costs in 2016, for example, exceeded well over one billion dollars, a circumstance that appeared to heighten the influence of wealthy interests.

Congress first sought to control the effects of money on elections in 1907 when it prohibited corporate contributions, but this restriction and others were rarely enforced. The first meaningful limits on campaign financing came in 1971, with establishment of the Federal Election Commission to regulate and monitor contributions and expenditures. The Watergate scandals following the election of 1972 led to even tighter limits in 1974. Two years later, in *Buckley v. Valeo* (1976), the Supreme Court rejected an argument that the restrictions controlled conduct rather than speech but decided that the First Amendment's protection of speech could be overcome by a compelling government interest in preventing corruption. However, the justices struck down limits on total campaign expenditures from a candidate's own funds, as well as any spending made independently by supporters, as unacceptable restraints on speech. The ruling dramatically increased the use of "soft money" by groups or individuals supportive of or opposed to a candidate.

Legislation in 2002, commonly known as the McCain-Feingold law, placed new limits on a variety of political activity, and extended the regulations to state parties in any election in which federal candidates appeared on the ballot. The Court upheld the law in 2003 as legitimate to protect the "integrity of the process," a standard more relaxed than the need to guard against narrowly defined corruption. This criterion changed dramatically in 2010, when the Supreme Court declared unconstitutional any statutory restrictions on campaign contributions made by corporations and unions (*Citizens United v. Federal Elections Commission*). The controversial decision, based on the First Amendment's guarantee of unrestricted political speech, overturned Court precedents and federal law dating to the Progressive Era. The congressional and presidential elections that followed unleashed a flood of campaign cash, much of it so-called dark money that did not need to be reported.

The story of political representation in modern America is more complicated than a simple narrative of wealth and special interests. Counterbalancing the *Citizens United* case is a decades-long increase in the use of direct democracy, such as initiative and referendum, to bypass reluctant or captured legislatures. In the 1970s and 1980s the trend was to limit property taxes but in the 1990s and first decade of the twenty-first century voters resorted to this device to address social issues such as same-sex marriage, abortion, the use of medical marijuana, environmental justice, and educational requirements, among other causes both conservative and liberal. These developments suggest that the nation's impulse remains toward more democracy.

The framers distrusted direct democracy, preferring instead the indirect form of a democratic republic, but the theories on which they based the Constitution, popular sovereignty and representation, had their own internal dynamic that pointed toward more, not less, citizen participation in government. Democracy was not the inevitable outcome of this citizen involvement, and in fact, democracy, as signified by the right to vote, came only after much resistance from interests bound by considerations of race, class, and gender. But ultimately it came and with such force that it redefined the Constitution and the nation.

Chapter 6
Equality

Equality was not an explicit core value of the Constitution, nor was it a basic condition of republican governments. The framers lived in a world based on class distinctions. They rejected hereditary aristocracy but casually accepted the idea of a natural aristocracy based on merit. Republican liberty existed to allow merit to flourish, not to create an unnatural order in which the capacities and talents of men counted for little.

Even so, political equality was an animating force of the Revolution—it is central to the Declaration of Independence—although this condition applied primarily to white men who owned property. But republicanism rejected any effort to promote inequality by law. The Constitution banned titles of nobility, as did the various state constitutions. This animus against privilege resulted in abolition of English laws that protected a landed, hereditary aristocracy. The removal of property requirements for voting, a product of the second wave of state constitution-making in the 1820s and 1830s, reflected this impulse as well. The embrace of democracy and market capitalism strengthened an ethic that accepted differences based on talent so long as men had the freedom to compete fairly.

Racial slavery hobbled any impulse toward a more positive expression of equality. The founding generation had made a bargain with slavery, and the three-fifths, fugitive slave, and slave trade clauses, among other pro-slavery markers in the Constitution, were powerful symbols of the limits of liberty and equality in 1787. The Constitution not only permitted slavery, but federalism and the extra-constitutional party system served to promote it. The Bill of Rights did not bind the states. Many states did not consider African Americans to be citizens, and southern states mandated a separate and inferior status for them. National citizenship was not available to blacks either, as the *Dred Scott* case made clear.

A persistent antislavery crusade challenged the constitutional and legal contract with slavery. From the late 1780s, reformers considered the Constitution corrupted by slavery and denounced its inconsistency with the Declaration of Independence. They found early success in abolishing slavery in northern states where slaveholders and blacks were few. The Northwest Ordinance of 1787, which prohibited slavery in the territories north of the Ohio River, further ensured that new states carved from this territory would be free states on their admission to the Union.

Sentiment for equality before the law for all races, however, was almost nonexistent. Universal male suffrage generally excluded free blacks, and many local and state laws restricted their access to housing, occupations, public schools, and even mobility. The Indiana Constitution of 1851, for instance, prohibited migration of African Americans into the state; other states in the Midwest required them to post bonds for good behavior. Most states in the North maintained segregated schools, banned interracial marriage, and denied blacks the right to serve on juries or to testify in a case in which a white person was a party. At best, equality before the law was the rule within legally recognized groups, not between whites and blacks.

Equality for white men only was too much at odds with American ideals to remain unchallenged. Abolitionist William Lloyd

Garrison condemned the Constitution as "a covenant with death and an agreement with Hell," but other antislavery advocates sought to reinterpret it to support the elimination of slavery. Gradualists wanted to use the commerce clause to ban the interstate slave trade and to interpret the Fifth Amendment's due process clause to include liberty of movement or the right to pursue an occupation.

A more radical antislavery constitutional argument was based on natural rights. The supremacy of natural law over man-made law had gained early endorsement from jurists who suggested that statutes in violation of natural law were illegitimate. The natural-rights argument was especially significant because it fused the nation's two founding documents, the Declaration of Independence and the Constitution. By this measure, the framers did not jettison the Declaration in favor of the Constitution; they never proposed "to accept the shell, and throw the kernel away." The Declaration was the standard for perfecting the Union, the goal announced in the Constitution's preamble.

The new Republican Party, formed in 1854, advanced antislavery constitutionalism as the proper expression of the nation's commitment to equality. Many Republicans agreed that native-born free blacks were state citizens and thereby under the protection of the Constitution. They embraced the Declaration's assertion of natural rights for all men as the foundation of republican government. This stance did not mean social and political equality for blacks—such a position would have been political suicide—but it did accept their right to liberty and to the equal protection of law.

The Civil War transformed American constitutionalism. By 1863, abolition had become a war aim, with the Emancipation Proclamation announcing black liberation as a moral imperative and military necessity. Although designed in part to weaken the Confederacy, the proclamation served as a bookend with the

Gettysburg Address to set forth a new constitutional framework, with equality at its center. The address notably redefined the Constitution in light of the Declaration of Independence, which Abraham Lincoln viewed as a timeless charter of universal principles. For Lincoln, the founding documents were inextricably linked: the Declaration's principle of equality ("liberty for all")," he wrote in 1861, was "the apple of gold," and the Constitution "the picture of silver." The Constitution was made "not to *conceal*, or *destroy* the apple but to *adorn*, and *preserve* it. The *picture* was made for the apple—not the apple for the picture."

What scholars call the second American Constitution had its roots in three amendments adopted between 1865 and 1870. The Thirteenth Amendment (1865) ended slavery and committed the nation to a principle of freedom for all residents. The Fourteenth Amendment (1868) set the terms of citizenship, an omission in the 1787 charter, and made state citizenship a consequence of national citizenship. It also made equality part of the constitutional vocabulary. The Fifteenth Amendment (1870) designated African American men as political equals (voters) in the national republic. All three amendments gave the federal government the power to enforce these new guarantees, which it did initially in a series of civil rights measures.

The Fourteenth Amendment became the keystone of a constitutional commitment to equality. Section 1 defined US citizenship, prevented states from excluding blacks from the benefits of state citizenship, and established guarantees for individual rights. Its language was pregnant with promise— states could not "make or enforce any law which shall abridge the privileges and immunities of citizens of the United States" or "deprive any person of life, liberty, or property without due process of law" or deny anyone "equal protection of the laws"—even if the meaning of these clauses was unclear. One thing was certain: equality of citizens under the law was now a constitutional requirement.

At first, the new order held. The Republican Congress passed laws to punish anyone who interfered with the right of blacks to vote and to suppress white terrorism that was rampant throughout the South. These acts provided individuals with a federal remedy against private acts of violence and used national power, including the army, to guarantee access to the ballot box. The Civil Rights Act of 1875 even asserted federal authority to ensure equality in public accommodations, a measure that struck directly at the idea of social segregation.

The 1875 measure marked the final stage of Reconstruction. Democrats regained political control in southern states, while Republicans became more cautious politically. The denouement came when the Supreme Court, citing federalism, circumscribed national power to protect civil rights and enforce equality. Following traditional practice, the justices allowed states wide discretion to protect individual liberty as they saw fit. It was not an unusual view. Suspicious of centralized power, Americans clung to the principle of local autonomy—and true to this ideal, the Court could not imagine that overcoming slavery warranted an extreme reallocation of governmental power.

The major interpretative hurdle for the Court was the relationship between national and state citizenship. It was a new issue; not until the Fourteenth Amendment did the Constitution identify who was a citizen of the United States. The amendment revived the traditional English rule of citizenship by birth, thereby overruling the *Dred Scott* decision that excluded blacks and Indians because of ethnicity. A direct connection now existed between all citizens and the federal government. But what was the relationship between the two kinds of citizenship, state and national?

In the *Slaughterhouse Cases* (1873), the Court's majority decided that the amendment had not changed the nature of the Union; it only added what had been omitted. A minority opinion by Justice

Stephen J. Field, however, was notably prophetic. In the original Constitution, Field argued, several provisions prohibited states from discriminating against citizens of other states, yet citizens were not protected from the misuse of power by their own state. The Fourteenth Amendment's recognition of national citizenship protected individuals from illegitimate actions of their own state government. Field's view was revolutionary—it rejected the assumptions of dual federalism—but not until much later did its potential for interpersonal equality become apparent.

Initially, the Court extended the logic of the *Slaughterhouse* majority in a series of decisions in the 1870s and 1880s, often with tragic consequences for black citizens. An early example in 1873 when armed whites in Colfax, Louisiana, massacred as many as one hundred freedmen who supported local Republican claims to office. The Supreme Court set aside the successful federal prosecutions for the crime. The Fourteenth Amendment, the justices concluded, did not empower the federal government to punish private individuals who violated the rights of other citizens. Later, the Court struck down the Civil Rights Act of 1875's ban on private discrimination in hotels, restaurants, and public transportation.

Equal protection, a Fourteenth Amendment guarantee, was left solely to the discretion of the states. The result was predictable— rigid segregation under Jim Crow laws and an official unwillingness to protect blacks from violence should they breach this social norm, especially in southern states. The Court officially acknowledged racial segregation in *Plessy v. Ferguson* (1896), in which it enshrined "separate but equal" as acceptable under the equal protection clause. Stripped of its common-sense meaning, equality for minorities under the Fourteenth Amendment was an empty promise.

Political and social changes made equality the central constitutional issue of the twentieth century. The Great Migration that began around 1910 brought more than one million African Americans to northern cities as industrial workers. They became members of powerful labor unions and an important part of big-city Democratic Party political machines. The New Deal made a place for black Americans, including them among its beneficiaries for poverty relief and providing professional jobs and opportunities for leadership. In response, African Americans abandoned the party of Abraham Lincoln for the party of Franklin Roosevelt. Public attitudes began to shift as well, thanks to research that undermined the myth of white superiority and to distaste for European regimes based on racial hatred.

At first, the Supreme Court did not incorporate the new perception of governmental responsibility into its decisions about racial equality. The justices unhesitatingly blocked state action that denied rights to blacks but were reluctant to intervene in private actions that had the same effect. For instance, they blocked a Missouri statute that sent black law students out of state to receive the same subsidy offered in-state white students, yet they accepted private actions such as restrictive covenants that resulted in residential segregation. The same circumstances prevailed in public schools, with both the Court and the federal government accepting racial separation as customary and legal.

The aftermath of World War II marked an important change in US race relations. Vital to both the armed forces and war-time industry, blacks became more militant. Protests and political action soon paid dividends. By the end of the 1940s, the national government was more active on behalf of African Americans than at any time since Reconstruction. The Justice Department vigorously pursued lynching and supported an NAACP effort to end restrictive covenants. President Harry Truman used his executive authority in 1948 to desegregate the military. The emergence of popular African American celebrities such as Louis Armstrong and Jackie Robinson also signaled a cultural shift toward acceptance.

Aware of changing public attitudes, the Court was increasingly receptive to civil rights claims. In 1944, the justices held that the Texas all-white primary constituted state action and therefore unconstitutional; they also declared restrictive covenants unenforceable violations of the equal protection clause. An assault on *Plessy v. Ferguson* soon followed, led by Thurgood Marshall, chief lawyer for the NAACP Legal Defense Fund (and later the nation's first African American justice). Finally, in *Brown v. Board of Education* (1954), the Warren Court unanimously ruled that segregation in public schools was "inherently unequal."

Brown v. Board of Education was a landmark decision, but it was not an unvarnished triumph. The decision provided no remedy, and the justices agreed to hear a sequel to *Brown* in 1955. It settled on a standard of "all deliberate speed" to guide federal district courts in implementing desegregation locally. Anything more forceful, the justices feared, would expose the Court's fatal weakness—it could not enforce its decisions without the support of Congress and the executive branch, neither of which favored immediate desegregation.

The concern was not misplaced. What followed was massive resistance, often violent, in response to judicial desegregation orders. White southern politicians revived the discredited mantle of "states' rights" to justify "segregation now, segregation tomorrow, segregation forever," as Alabama governor George C. Wallace vowed. Legal segregation was no longer constitutional, but racial equality was not yet a constitutional reality. Ultimately federal troops were required to intervene in places like Little Rock, Oxford, and Tuscaloosa to assure compliance, but segregation remained the norm across the South—and at times elsewhere—until the late 1960s.

Brown made a difference in the way that Americans thought about race and equality, however. It directed public attention to the discrepancy between the Constitution in theory and the

6. Following the Supreme Court's ruling on racial desegregation in the late 1950s, schools such as Anacostia High School in Washington, DC, were integrated—often by busing in students from distant neighborhoods.

Constitution in practice and forced people to judge local customs against American ideals. No major political party endorsed a return to pre-*Brown* days, and public opinion polls showed most citizens viewed racial discrimination as morally wrong. *Brown* also motivated black citizens to extend its principle to other areas of life. The Montgomery, Alabama, bus boycott, a catalytic event in the modern history of civil rights, was a direct result of the decision, as were lunch counter sit-ins and freedom rides. *Brown* taught a valuable lesson: litigation alone was insufficient to bring about change; constitutional equality depended upon a social and political movement.

The civil rights movement of the 1960s cemented black equality as a matter of law, although not always of practice. Attempts to register black voters from 1961 to 1965 and civil rights marches met increasingly violent responses. The use of police attack dogs, the bombing of a black church in Alabama that killed four young schoolgirls, Klan murders of civil rights activists in Mississippi, and police brutality against marchers in Selma, Alabama, finally repelled the nation and provided the opportunity for President Lyndon B. Johnson to demand a congressional remedy for racial injustice.

Three important measures followed. The Civil Rights Act of 1964, which the Supreme Court upheld unanimously later that year, used an expansive interpretation of the commerce clause to end legal segregation in public accommodations, including entertainment venues. The act also banned employment discrimination on the basis of race, color, religion, national origin, or gender and halted federal funds to any program that did not adopt anti-discrimination policies. The Voting Rights Act of 1965 appointed federal examiners to monitor state and local voter registration and elections and ended state poll taxes, which the Twenty-Fourth Amendment had outlawed the previous year in federal elections. Significantly, these acts allowed the federal government to prosecute private discrimination, thus freeing Congress to protect individual rights more broadly.

By the late 1960s, urban race riots, black nationalism, and demands for economic equality divided the civil rights movement and soured white willingness to address past wrongs. A more conservative Court in the 1970s led by Warren E. Burger, chief justice from 1969 to 1986, slowed but did not abandon the revolution in civil rights; the justices no longer were united on their reading of what the Constitution allowed. They accepted busing as a remedy for school desegregation but refused to extend urban desegregation decrees to suburban areas without evidence of discriminatory intent. The Burger Court also interpreted the 1964 Civil Rights Act to forbid disparate impact in employment but ruled that laws lacking an explicit racial classification scheme would not receive strict scrutiny.

These decisions did not signal a retreat on civil rights as much as they did the emergence of more complex issues. From the mid-1970s, no popular consensus existed on what else constituted racial discrimination or what actions were required to correct past wrongs. Affirmative action programs in higher education made special allowances, including set-aside programs, for members of underrepresented groups, despite wide public opposition. The justices approved such programs but banned explicit racial quotas unless there was a history of discrimination. Elsewhere, the Court signaled that it was unwilling to accept more aggressive measures under the banner of equal protection. In 2007, it ruled that local school districts could not use race as a tiebreaker in assigning students to a school to achieve racial balance. "The way to stop discrimination on the basis of race is to stop discriminating on the basis of race," insisted Chief Justice John Roberts, who was appointed chief justice in 2005. The minority justices sharply criticized the decision, arguing that the constitutional mandate of racial equality at times required the explicit use of race-based criteria to overcome discrimination.

For many citizens, race mattered less in the last decades of the twentieth century and the first decade of the twenty-first century than at any time in the nation's history. Polls revealed a strong belief in the value of racial and ethnic diversity and the casual acceptance of racial integration among younger people. The election of an African American as president in 2008 also suggested that the United States had in fact achieved the constitutional equality promised by the Reconstruction amendments. If so, it was an uneasy triumph. Race still looms large in contemporary society, with blacks ranking low on most measures of social and economic progress. But most Americans no longer considered this disparity a constitutional problem.

The same was not true of other forms of inequality. All men in theory could claim rights under the Constitution; no woman could. For women, this situation was intolerable. From the middle of the nineteenth century, they pressed for equality with men, often relying on racism to justify their claim to equality: why

7. Many Americans believed that the Supreme Court's 1978 decision in *Regents of the University of California v. Bakke*, in which it ruled that the University of California at Davis could not bar Allan Bakke from its medical school on the basis of racial preferences, was a case of reverse discrimination. The ruling divided Americans over the issue of equal opportunity.

should poor, ignorant black men have rights denied to educated white women? These prejudices distracted women reformers from attacking the social assumptions that blocked their progress. Granting equality to women threatened to change society fundamentally by upsetting the legal dominance of husbands over their wives, which was at the heart of domestic and economic relationships. For decades, white Americans, male or female, resisted this possibility.

The successful attacks on racial discrimination was not lost on women, who looked both to legislation and to the Fourteenth Amendment's equal protection clause as ways to remove gender-based inequities. In 1920, the women's movement scored a major victory with the ratification of the Nineteenth Amendment forbidding discrimination in suffrage based on sex, and yet the expected transformation of American life (and the promised purification of politics) did not occur. Women largely voted in much the same way that men did.

World War II spurred changes that a constitutional amendment did not. As men went to war, women took their place in factories and government, achieving an economic independence that they had lacked as non-working wives. They also entered college and the professions in increasing numbers. But new opportunities for women too often did not lead to equality with men in matters of pay, working conditions, or career advancement. The 1964 Civil Rights Act pointed to a potential solution. It outlawed discrimination based on sex as well as race, an addition made by southern opponents to weaken the bill. The statute also established the Equal Opportunities Employment Commission (EEOC) and empowered it to investigate workplace discrimination. The national government now had tools to bring about change, albeit incrementally.

Many women wanted more progress, more quickly. They sought comprehensive change and believed that only a constitutional amendment could bring it about. This conclusion was not new. The campaign to add gender equality to the Constitution had begun soon after the adoption of the Nineteenth Amendment, which had done nothing to change the vast legal framework limiting the roles of women in other areas of American life.

In 1923, militant suffragists proposed an Equal Rights Amendment (ERA) but made little progress toward enacting it. By the 1960s, a more aggressive and more political women's movement pushed for changes in state laws and, with the aid of the American Civil Liberties Union (ACLU), challenged gender-discrimination practices in state and federal courts. Advocates also sought ratification of a revised ERA, which used language that tracked the Fourteenth and Fifteenth Amendments: "Equality of rights under the law shall not be denied or abridged by the United States or by any State on account of sex." Feminists considered an amendment necessary to make the law clear, to place the burden on government to justify any legal distinction between men and women, and to make the principle of gender equality permanent.

Congress passed the Equal Rights Amendment in 1972 but the measure failed by three states to achieve ratification upon its deadline ten years later. The amendment met resistance from conservatives, including many women, who claimed it would mean unacceptable social changes such as gay marriages and women in combat. The campaign for the ERA also failed because the Court undermined the impetus for an amendment by changing the standard it used to assess claims of sex discrimination.

The shift began with a 1971 decision that deemed an Idaho law irrational by automatically preferring men over women as executors of decedents' estates. Two years later the justices dismantled the law's assumption of female dependency in marriage. Finally, in 1976, the Court adopted a standard of "intermediate scrutiny" to evaluate laws that differentiated between men and women. This rule, still in use in gender discrimination cases, was less than the strict scrutiny standard applied to issues of race, which required a compelling government interest to justify legal distinctions, but it was a burden of proof that many states could not meet.

Congress responded by prohibiting practices that the Court previously had found permissible. When the Court determined that discrimination against pregnant workers was not unconstitutional, for example, Congress made it illegal. With few exceptions, sex discrimination by law had disappeared by the 1990s, symbolized by a Supreme Court decision that Virginia could not deny admission to women at the state-supported Virginia Military Institute.

The ERA had not succeeded, but the cause of women's legal equality had. The membership of the Court itself confirmed the shift: Sandra Day O'Connor became the first woman justice on the Supreme Court in 1981, followed by Ruth Bader Ginsburg as the second in 1993. With the appointments in 2009 and 2010 of Sonia Sotomayor and Elena Kagan, respectively, one-third of the Court is now female, O'Connor having retired in 2006.

The movement toward constitutional equality left areas in which legal discrimination was possible. Equality for gays and lesbians was the new battleground, with marriage becoming its central focus. Traditionally, legal marriage has been the exclusive domain of heterosexual couples, and it had a preferred status under many federal and state laws. But American culture was becoming increasingly comfortable with gays and lesbians in highly visible roles, especially in entertainment, and legal change soon followed.

By the turn of the twenty-first century, demands for full equality for LGBT citizens, which had begun in New York City's Stonewall riots of 1969, resulted in significant changes. Supreme courts in six states invalidated heterosexual-only marriage laws as violations of the equal protection clauses of their state constitutions; and in 2009 Vermont and New Hampshire became the first states to make gay marriage legal by statute. More than thirty states opposed these changes by amending their constitutions to ban gay unions, which federal courts invalidated after a 2013 Supreme Court decision that a federal law restricting marriage to heterosexual couples violated the Fourteenth Amendment. Within two years same-sex marriage was lawful in two-thirds of the states, and in 2015 the Court ruled in *Obergefell v. Hodges* that state-level bans on same-sex marriage were unconstitutional.

Equality became a constitutional value because of angry, insistent demands by Americans on the margins of public life who believed the Declaration of Independence applied to them as well. Amendments to the nation's charter have been the principal vehicles for this change, but the promises contained in them, especially in the Fourteenth Amendment, were realized slowly. The touchstone of this transformation—due process of law and equal protection of laws—was sufficiently flexible to allow reformers to push for new meanings and for opponents to resist by invoking tradition.

The pattern was familiar because it was the path used to make the Constitution more democratic. What often goes unrecognized, however, is how these amendments, based on principles of democracy and equality, have changed the nature of the Constitution itself. The first ten amendments pitted liberty versus power; they had restrained government to protect individual liberty. The new amendments made power the friend of liberty and government the guarantor of freedom. In doing so, they created a new constitution in which guarantees of liberty and equality fulfilled the revolutionary pledges of 1776. It is this constitution that Americans now use to determine what these promises mean in their ordinary lives.

Chapter 7
Rights

Throughout American history, rights have been invented and repudiated, fought over and striven for, expanded and violated. From the nation's beginnings revolutionaries appealed to natural rights they enjoyed not by their birth as Englishmen but by their humanity. It allowed rights to be claimed without limit if men agreed to them. The abstract character of natural rights gave them a protean quality—there was no limit to their growth—but it also made them a matter of contention. The question often became which rights and for whom? The resulting argument about rights became nothing less than an argument about the meaning of liberty itself.

Rights were part of fundamental law in almost every state in 1776. The goal in recognizing such rights was to protect liberty and promote the public good. This was not the stuff of unrestrained individualism. It was instead a civic republicanism that emphasized individual liberty within the context of community and citizen participation in government.

By 1787, however, concerns about democratic excesses had eroded utopian hopes for maximizing liberty through the growth of public virtue. For the framers, liberty required structural restraints on power but the ratification debates produced another condition: written acknowledgment of the rights individuals could claim against the general government. The federal Bill of Rights (the first ten amendments to the Constitution) contained twenty-five assorted substantive and procedural rights, many already having found some expression, although not universally, in the various state constitutions and declarations of rights.

The First Amendment, the only one to begin with the words "Congress shall make no law," contained guarantees concerning speech, religion, press, assembly, and petition. These rights allowed citizens to participate in public life and to maintain a private faith, free from interference by government. The next two amendments restrained the central government from interfering with an individual's right to bear arms (Second) and from commandeering private homes to house troops (Third). The five amendments that follow (Fourth through Eighth) outlined procedural guarantees for individuals who confronted the power of government, usually as persons accused of crimes. The Fourth and Sixth Amendments, for example, established detailed requirements for arrest and trial, while the Eighth Amendment forbade cruel and unusual punishments, including excessive fines.

The Ninth and Tenth Amendments are more general but they too set boundaries on the power of the central government. The Ninth recognized the potential for additional rights by commanding that the "enumeration in the Constitution of certain rights shall not be construed to deny or disparage others retained by the people." This language reinforced the notion of popular sovereignty and the contractual nature of rights; it also opened the door for the judicial discovery of rights, especially in the twentieth century. The Tenth sought to safeguard rights by reserving rights not specifically identified to the States or to the people. It too was a source of litigation, often unsuccessful, as the role of the national government expanded during the twentieth century.

Almost from the moment of their ratification, the rights promised in the new constitutional amendments came into dispute. When faced with practical problems, people disagreed about what government could and could not do. The sharp political divisions of the 1790s, especially the emergence of a highly partisan press, exposed the matter plainly. Party newspapers engaged in vicious personal attacks and routinely challenged the integrity of government officials. The Federalists viewed this development with alarm, and they used their control of Congress to pass the Sedition Act of 1798, which allowed prosecution of individuals who criticized the government, officials, or laws in a manner designed to bring them into disrepute or to cause a civil disturbance.

Under the cultural and political logic of the period, the act was an effort to reconcile the competing demands of power and liberty. Federalists believed that vindictive attacks on the general government would fatally undermine the popular support it needed to survive. But by modern standards, the act was a blatant attempt to suppress speech: prosecutions under the act were strictly partisan. The law expired in 1801 without a definitive judicial interpretation, but it was clear, nonetheless, that the founding generation had sharp differences of opinion about the scope of free speech and free press in practice.

The concern for rights became more intense after the Revolution, although the focus shifted from federal to state governments. In 1833, the US Supreme Court determined that the Bill of Rights restrained the federal government alone, a rule that held sway until the twentieth century. This decision had a limited effect because almost every state constitution included the federal rights, and some exceeded them. But the decision also meant that the interpretation of rights could vary widely from state to state.

Religion was especially problematic for individual rights. The absence of an official religion led to intense competition for adherents among faith groups, which promoted diversity and tolerance. But these values rested on a shared Protestant culture.

Law reflected this belief. Legislatures enacted anti-blasphemy statutes and Sunday closing laws, local school broads required religious instruction, and local governments enacted temperance legislation based explicitly on evangelical Protestant doctrines about alcohol. Courts upheld these measures and were rarely sympathetic to complaints from Catholics, Jews, and adherents of other faiths about their discriminatory impact.

In the few religion cases the US Supreme Court considered in the nineteenth century, the justices drew a line between belief, which the government could not touch, and action, which was legitimate for government to regulate or prohibit. In 1878, for example, the justices rejected the argument that the Mormon doctrine of polygamy was protected against state action. The decision unleashed a flood of anti-polygamy legislation in the states, and Congress required Utah to adopt such a statute to gain admission to the Union, which happened in 1890. The relationship of the government to religion was circumscribed by the conviction proclaimed by the Supreme Court in an 1892 decision that stated: "This is a Christian nation."

Even though applied unevenly to religious and ethnic minorities, the goal of expansive, liberal rights maintained a powerful hold on Americans throughout the nineteenth century. The antebellum reform movements especially sought to extend rights to excluded groups. Women made their case for voting rights and property rights expressed in language borrowed from the Declaration of Independence. Workingmen invoked "inalienable rights" to lobby for fair wages and the ability to use their free time as they saw fit. Reformers placed the revolutionary concept of natural rights, especially equal rights, at the center of their campaigns, although most reformers limited its benefits to white men.

The movement to abolish slavery had a profound effect on rights as we know them today. It linked equality and rights for all men, not only whites, as a matter of justice and morality. Northern states never extended first-class citizenship to African Americans but neither did they deprive blacks of individual rights because of their color. The crusade for rights even extended to fugitive slaves. Personal liberty laws—statutes that extended due process to runaways—symbolized an expansive culture of individual rights that by the 1840s and 1850s had become a hallmark of American society outside the slaveholding South.

The adoption of three constitutional amendments during Reconstruction marked the zenith of a second wave of rights invention. Each added new constitutional guarantees, and the Fourteenth Amendment contained the seeds of a rights revolution by changing the traditional relationship of national and state governments. Significantly, its guarantees of equal protection and due process of law extended to all persons rather than to men. Fairness and equal treatment under law was now a fundamental obligation owed by the United States to anyone within its jurisdiction.

For the first time, the federal government had the responsibility to protect the rights of individuals—at least in theory. Yet federal courts rarely interpreted the amendment in this way during the last half of the nineteenth century. The Supreme Court held that the amendment did not require states and local governments to respect the guarantees of the federal Bill of Rights. The justices instead followed traditional practice and allowed states wide discretion to protect individual liberty as they saw fit. Most Americans accepted this view. The voices of protests came most often from marginalized groups, notably women and blacks, who struggled to change cultural and legal norms.

By the end of the nineteenth century, the Fourteenth Amendment had assumed a new role as protector of corporate property rights. In 1886, the Supreme Court recognized corporations as persons for purposes of the Fourteenth Amendment and then interpreted the amendment to protect freedom of contract, an inferred individual right, from state interference. (Individual rights noted explicitly in the Constitution, such as freedom of speech, were not included, although later Courts would take this step.) This stance prevented most state and federal regulation of economic activity in the name of protecting individual liberty.

But in one case, the Court provided a wedge into the Fourteenth Amendment that later would prove decisive in extending the Bill of Rights to the states. When Chicago paid a railroad company only a dollar for the use of its property, the Court ruled that it violated the Fifth Amendment's requirement of just compensation, which the justices deemed to be included in the due process clause of the Fourteenth Amendment. It marked the first time that the Court incorporated a guarantee from the Bill of Rights into the Fourteenth Amendment's restraint on states (*Chicago, Burlington, and Quincy Railroad v. Chicago*, 1897). Although economic liberty was the cause in this case, incorporation would become the major vehicle for a nationalization of rights in the twentieth century.

Increasingly, progressive reformers asked whether other safeguards of the Bill of Rights were included substantively—were they incorporated?—in the Fourteenth Amendment's due process and equal protection clauses. World War I and its aftermath presented an opportunity to test this question when the federal government sought to suppress dissent as harmful to the war effort.

State courts long had refused to protect radical or offensive speech, as well as speech accompanied by action that threatened public order. At first the Supreme Court followed this tradition: it upheld convictions under state laws of anti-war protestors, including Socialist Party presidential candidate (Eugene V. Debs), because the First Amendment did not protect speech that presented "a clear and present danger." By 1925, however, the Court had changed its mind, ruling for the first time that the

8. Lewis Hine's photograph of child labor on the overnight shift of a glass factory in Indiana helped to spur progressive state and federal legislation on who could work, for how long, and under what conditions. These laws met resistance in federal courts, which relied on the commerce clause and liberty of contract to blunt such governmental regulation of economic relationships. The US Supreme Court finally accepted national oversight of working conditions when it judged the Fair Labor Standards Act of 1938 as constitutional.

Fourteenth Amendment protected freedoms of speech and press from impairment by the states (*Gitlow v. New York*). It would be several years before the full impact of this decision become apparent, but it marked the beginning of a new era for individual rights. The question of incorporation—whether guarantees of the Bill of Rights were included in the due process clause of the Fourteenth Amendment as protection against state governments— soon would become one of the great constitutional issues of the twentieth century.

By the late 1930s the justices were marching toward the nationalization of First Amendment rights. In 1937 and 1938 they ruled that all First Amendment guarantees were incorporated into the Fourteenth Amendment's due process clause; these rights,

Justice Benjamin Cardozo wrote, were "the matrix, the indispensable condition" for nearly all other freedoms. Other rights were subject to selective incorporation, or inclusion one by one in the meaning of due process. Here, the Court would apply only those rights that are "of the very essence of a scheme of ordered liberty" and could be considered fundamental because they were so deeply rooted in American traditions (*Palko v. Connecticut*, 1937). This standard meant that the justices would consider individual rights on a case-by-case basis, with strict scrutiny applied to laws that appeared to cut harshly against minorities.

The new standard invited judges to use their discretion; it also divided the Court. Two justices embodied the split. Felix Frankfurter favored selective incorporation. Although politically progressive, the former Harvard law dean insisted that the Constitution contained historically determined principles that the judge must apply carefully but always with deference to the decisions of popularly elected representatives. Justice Hugo Black took an opposite stance. A New Deal politician from Alabama, Black insisted on the total incorporation of the Bill of Rights under the Fourteenth Amendment. As a US senator, he had been appalled at the Court's defense of corporations under the doctrine of substantive due process. Total incorporation, he believed, would force the Court to recognize that the whole Bill of Rights restrained state and local governments, not simply whichever clauses the justices chose to include.

The Frankfurter-Black dispute framed the debate over incorporation for the next three decades, yet it scarcely had begun when World War II and the Cold War plunged the Court into a debate about how far individual rights extended in times of threat. The first test involved Jehovah's Witnesses, a religious group that claimed First Amendment protection for their children's refusal to salute the flag in school as required by state laws. Initially the justices deferred to legislative judgments that

Rights

encouraging patriotism justified a minor interference with religious belief. But several justices reconsidered after public attacks on the Witnesses, and, in 1943, the Court ruled that the First Amendment protected freedom of religion from state infringement. If there was any "fixed star in our constitution," Justice Robert Jackson wrote, "it is that no official, high or petty, can prescribe what shall be orthodox in politics, nationalism, religion, or other matters of opinion or force citizens to confess by word or act their faith therein" (*West Virginia State Board of Education v. Barnette*, 1943).

The assault on liberty by the Axis powers during World War II renewed belief by Americans in the necessity of individual rights. President Roosevelt reminded the nation of the need to protect essential human freedoms, and his call for a second Bill of Rights included new guarantees, such as the right to a home, adequate medical care, and old age insurance, among others. But such talk was not always consistent with rights in action. Several weeks after the Japanese attack on Pearl Harbor, Roosevelt ordered the relocation of Japanese American citizens into internment camps. The executive order violated the equal protection and due process clauses of the Fourteenth Amendment, but the Supreme Court upheld the actions, unwilling to challenge the president's claim of national security despite the lack of evidence of a real threat. (Later scholarship demonstrated that the government altered the record to mislead the justices.) In times of crisis, concerns about national security generally trumped individual rights.

Following World War II, the exposure of domestic spy rings and the communist takeover of Eastern Europe and China persuaded national and state governments to launch massive loyalty programs to purge communist sympathizers. At first the Supreme Court supported convictions under these laws, even though they punished beliefs, not actions. Once public hysteria subsided in the mid-1950s, however, the justices reverted to a more liberal interpretation of these safeguards. They operated under the

Minersville, Pa.
Nov. 5, 1935

Our School Directors
Dear Sirs
I do not salute the flag be-
cause I have promised to do
the will of God. That means
that I must not worship anything
out of harmony with God's law.
In the twentieth chapter of
Exodus it is stated, "Thou shalt
not make unto thee any graven
image nor bow down to them nor
serve them for I the Lord thy God
am a jealous God visiting the in-
iquity of the fathers upon the children

9. In a letter to the Minersville, Pennsylvania, school administration, ten-year-old Billy Gobitas explained his refusal to salute the flag, writing, "I do not salute the flag because I have promised to do the will of God."

increasingly accepted view that the due process and equal protection clauses of the Fourteenth Amendment applied to the states as well as the federal government. What remained to be decided were what liberties these clauses included under their protection.

In the 1950s, acting with unprecedented boldness, the Warren Court promoted a new understanding of individual rights. The reforms came so swiftly that many commentators labeled them as revolutionary—and in a sense, they were. What had changed was the willingness of the justices to broaden individual rights aggressively in areas where legislatures traditionally had set standards. The Court mandated sweeping reforms of the electoral process, political representation, school desegregation, religious freedom and separation of church and state, obscenity, and free speech, among others, all based on new interpretations of constitutional guarantees.

Free speech was a bellwether for the expanded conception of rights. In 1919, the Court had adopted the rule of "clear and present danger," a refinement of the previous bad tendency standard, for judging the constitutionality of speech. A half-century later, the justices adopted a different test: government cannot regulate the content of speech unless it is likely to incite or produce imminent lawless action. With few exceptions—"fighting words" and obscenity, for example—speech enjoyed the protection of the First Amendment.

The modern Court has applied this doctrine to expressive speech as well, for instance, accepting flag-burning as protected. But this standard does not mean that regulation is never acceptable. Commercial speech and low-value speech, such as pornography, have fewer protections, but they too are within the First Amendment's orbit. Political speech is beyond government control, even if regulation seeks to ensure the equality of voices in public debate. This standard explains, in part, the Court's controversial opinions in *Citizens United v. Federal Election Commission* (2010), in which the justices struck down congressional limits on campaign spending by individuals, groups, and corporations, even though the decision made it easier for wealthy interests to drown out other voices.

Few decisions met more continuing criticism than ones involving religion, in part because they affected the beliefs and practices of millions of faithful Americans. The most controversial decisions came in the 1960s, when the Warren Court overturned prescribed nondenominational prayer and required Bible readings in public schools. Newspaper headlines, as well as Protestant and Catholic leaders, decried the rulings as un-American. Relying on Thomas Jefferson's argument that the First Amendment erected a "wall of separation" between church and state, the Court did not retreat: state mandates involving religion were unconstitutional, even when the aim was not explicitly religious. It struck down an Arkansas law, for instance, requiring equal time be given to creationist views when teaching evolution in public schools. But the Court accommodated other laws that affected religious practice, such as when it accepted Sunday closing laws as constitutional.

Rights of the accused also were fertile—and controversial—ground for the expansion of individual liberties. Between 1961 and 1969 the Warren Court applied virtually all the procedural guarantees of the Bill of Rights to the states' administration of criminal justice. Some cases evoked little public concern, as when the Court extended the right of counsel, at state expense, to indigent defendants charged with serious crimes (*Gideon v. Wainwright*, 1963). More contentious decisions set new standards for search and seizure, broadened the exclusionary rule that barred illegally seized evidence to include state prosecutions, and nationalized the Sixth Amendment right of an accused to confront a witness against him. The justices even extended these rights to the nation's police stations and jails, places previously thought to be subject to local control only. The result was a national standard that governed all criminal proceedings at both federal and state levels.

Critics charged that the expansion of these rights favored criminals over public safety, although the decisions were more controversial when the accused was black, poor, or Hispanic. *Miranda v.*

Arizona (1966) was the cause célèbre of the new constitutional order. At issue was the Fifth Amendment's protection against self-incrimination. In *Miranda*, the justices required police to warn suspects of their right in language now well known to all Americans, thanks to countless television crime dramas. The criticism was immediate and sharp, but the conclusion that the Court had handcuffed the police proved to be greatly exaggerated. Later studies revealed that less than 1 percent of all convictions had to be overturned for failure to issue the warning.

The 1960s expansion of rights was troublesome to many people, but more problematic were new rights that the justices inferred—invented, critics complained—from constitutional language. Chief among these implied rights was the right to privacy, which the Constitution does not mention explicitly. Initially, privacy meant the right to be secure in one's home. By the twentieth century, new technologies—for example, the ability to tap phone conversations—allowed law officers to breach the sanctity of the home without trespassing on physical space. In 1928 the Court ruled that wiretapping required no warrant, but the dissent by Justice Louis Brandeis pointed to a different future. The Fourth and Fifth Amendments, he wrote, "conferred, against the Government, the right to be let alone—the most comprehensive of rights and the one most valued by civilized men" (*Olmstead v. United States*).

Four decades later, in *Griswold v. Connecticut* (1965), the Court adopted this standard when it rejected a state law that banned contraceptives and prevented anyone from encouraging their use. For the majority, Justice William O. Douglas found the right to privacy in various guarantees designed to create "zones of privacy," such as the Third Amendment's ban on quartering soldiers in private homes, the Fourth Amendment's explicit recognition of the right of people to be secure in their homes, and the Fifth Amendment's self-incrimination clause. Others found a constitutional basis for privacy in the Ninth Amendment's recognition of unnamed rights retained by the people.

Although the result in *Griswold* was not controversial, the way it was reached suggested a liberal judicial activism reminiscent of an earlier conservative activism. It raised questions not only about the proper interpretation of the Constitution but also whether judicial decisions could establish new rights. The controversy intensified with the Court's decision in *Roe v. Wade* (1973), which guaranteed a woman's right to abortion based on a right to privacy. The continuing, often rancorous, debate over abortion demonstrates how contentious the claims of a court-discovered right of personal autonomy can be, even in a society otherwise dedicated to individualism.

By the late 1960s, the remarkable expansion of individual rights was nearing an end. The decade's turbulent history of urban riots, political violence, and rising crime rates undermined public support for Warren Court reforms, which became a major issue in the 1968 presidential election. The winning candidate, Richard M. Nixon, promised to reverse the trend toward greater liberalization of individual rights. Subsequent elections also featured this theme, with Ronald Reagan in 1980 and 1984 making a similar pledge to stop the creation of "judge-made rights."

Three successive chief justices, Warren E. Burger, William H. Rehnquist, and John Roberts, all appointed by Republican presidents, held similar views, but the courts they led left much of the Warren Court's legacy in place. The justices did not abandon the new-found catalogue of rights but focused instead on what these rights meant in practice. In matters of religion, for example, the Burger Court evoked a three-pronged test to determine when government action violated the establishment clause: it must have a secular purpose; its impact must be primarily secular; and it must create an excessive entanglement between the state and religion (*Lemon v. Kurtzman*, 1971). Under the *Lemon* test, the Court banned officially sanctioned prayers at public high school events and rejected public financial aid to religious schools, but it also has allowed tax-supported vouchers to support school choice, including private religious schools.

These cases revealed a Court grappling with how to accommodate religious belief with the demands of a highly pluralistic and increasingly secular society. A similar dilemma confronted the justices as they defined other rights for a society experiencing a flood of legal and illegal immigration, rapid changes in communication technologies, and a new ethic of personal autonomy. The Court at times has reaffirmed explicitly what had once been viewed as a radical decision, for example, by upholding *Miranda* warnings. In other areas, the justices went beyond the 1960s decisions to expand or uphold individual liberties, especially the rights of women and affirmative action programs designed to remedy racial discrimination.

Affirmative action especially raised the question of whether group rights are constitutionally protected. What began as an effort to correct long-standing discrimination against blacks soon moved into new rights claims for other groups—women, gays and lesbians, ethnic minorities, and the disabled, among others. Social welfare rights—right to a job, health care, or education, among others—were especially prominent in this more recent rights revolution. Significantly, most demands were pursued in the political arena and through the legislative process, both at state and federal levels, and not through the courts. The Americans with Disabilities Act of 1990, for instance, established legal rights for physically and mentally handicapped citizens, and the Patient Protection and Affordable Care Act of 2010 advanced the case for a right to universal access to health care.

Not all claims were accepted by courts, legislatures, or voters, however, and moving them successfully to constitutional protection proved difficult. In the 1970s, women's rights advocates pushed hard for an Equal Rights Amendment, only to fall short. Ironically, the political appeal of group or collectivist rights may have helped to secure the rights revolution by increasing the number of citizens and organizations invested in protecting its gains. But its ultimate constitutional success remained questionable because it stands at odds with the nation's deep historical and cultural commitment to individual rights.

Americans remain divided over how far their rights extend. New assertions of rights historically have met resistance and angry backlash. In many ways, this conflict has made rights talk even more contagious. Rights claims, after all, are made by someone who alleges a denial of liberty by the government or someone else. It is hard to think in terms of common values or community when engaged in rights talk; too much focus on individual liberties can skew our sense of the interests we hold in common. Yet what is most striking about the conflict over rights has been its democratic character. Rights are always a matter of public debate about the proper balance between order and liberty. It is a conversation that engaged the framers of the Constitution, and, as has been the case with each successive generation, Americans are continually working out the boundaries of those specific individual liberties that are essential for a just and free society.

Chapter 8
Security

Armed conflict poses an imminent threat to the nation's existence, but so does suspension of the nation's fundamental laws. The framers wrestled with how to grant government the power to defend the nation without providing it the means to threaten liberty. The question it raises—Does war suspend the Constitution or does the Constitution control the conduct of the war?—has rarely been absent from American history.

The framers gave Congress alone the power to declare war and set the rules for its conduct. Such an extraordinary action, they decided, must have the people's consent. This power extended to actions short of a declared war, as when Congress authorized reprisals in 1798 against the French naval attacks on American shipping, an action that the Supreme Court affirmed in 1801. The founding generation agreed that Congress decided matters of war, declared or not.

What seemed to be a clear mandate soon became murkier. Before 1860, Congress declared war only twice, in the War of 1812 and the Mexican War, but early presidents on occasion relied upon their role as commander-in-chief to protect American interests, seeking congressional approval only later. With Congress out of session, President Thomas Jefferson dispatched a naval squadron to protect American shipping in the Mediterranean and gave its commander blanket authority to destroy pirate ships from Tripoli. He concluded that circumstances sometimes required the president to "assume authorities beyond the law" in keeping with "the laws of necessity, of self-preservation, of saving our country when in danger." It was a justification hesitantly invoked in the nineteenth century; it became a mainstay in the twentieth.

The Civil War tested the war powers doctrine. Congress vigorously asserted constitutional power not only to win the war but to reshape the nation, concluding that the necessary and proper clause gave broad scope to its delegated powers to declare war, raise an army, and guarantee republican governments. This expansive reading allowed Congress to compel military service, take control of the nation's railroads and telegraph system, dredge canals and channel rivers, subsidize the creation of universities, and directly control the functions of seceding states, all measures deemed necessary to ensure victory.

As commander-in-chief, Abraham Lincoln also relied upon an aggressive, innovative, and controversial constitutionalism in the exercise of his power. He went beyond the Constitution in some instances and ignored its clear injunction in others. In 1861 he committed troops as head of the armed forces; spent funds Congress had not appropriated; ordered a blockade, an act of war; seized private property for military purposes; and called for the mobilization of 75,000 troops from state militias. Once conflict began, he unilaterally declared martial law in certain areas, closed the post office to treasonable mail, emancipated slaves, arrested people without a warrant, and tried civilians in military courts.

In justification, Lincoln relied on the presidential oath of office requiring him "to preserve, protect and defend the Constitution," as well as his role as commander-in-chief. He also invoked the Preamble, which delegated no powers but instead announced the aim to create a "more perfect union." The nation existed before the Constitution, Lincoln argued, and therefore had inherent authority over all subjects within the nation's borders. His primary responsibility was to safeguard the nation and fulfill his obligation to defend the Constitution.

Critics denounced Lincoln's actions as unconstitutional, and some scholars later joined the chorus. The charge seems exaggerated. Lincoln went well beyond limits accepted by his predecessors, but he later sought congressional approval. He also invited Congress to participate in the planning of military strategy, although constitutionally the role was his alone. These steps helped to insulate Lincoln politically and often legally. When considering challenges to his actions, the Supreme Court generally held that the president had broad executive power to defend the nation.

The Court was not so deferential after hostilities ended, especially on questions of civil liberty. In 1863, Congress retroactively authorized Lincoln's suspension of habeas corpus but ordered that prisoners be released if grand juries failed to indict them. Late in 1864 a military court sentenced Lambdin D. Milligan, a convicted traitor, to hang even though civil courts were open and operating. Upon appeal, the Supreme Court unanimously agreed that war did not suspend the Constitution, which "covers with the shield of its protection all classes of men, at all times, and under all circumstances," Justice David Davis, a Lincoln appointee, wrote (Ex parte *Milligan*, 1866).

The decision was a landmark decision for civil liberties, but it proved to be a thin reed of support during times of war. Courts throughout American history traditionally have refused to second-guess decisions based on claims of military necessity. The Civil War confirmed that Congress and the president could exercise power beyond the bounds of the Constitution if it was necessary to protect the nation.

The twentieth-century experience shifted this authority increasingly to the executive branch. World War I marked the beginning of this change. It was total war, fought on a global stage with mechanized armies and death on a grand scale, and it tested both the extent of federal power and the ability of Congress to respond quickly to its demands.

Soon after US entry into the war in 1917, Congress gave the president virtually unlimited power to regulate the entire economy in support of the war effort. The Lever Act marked a significant change in the constitutional conduct of war by delegating broad administrative authority to the president to run the war and to manage the nation's economy. The requirements of modern warfare overrode the constitutional separation and balance of powers, as well as the division of authority between national and state governments. This understanding soon became the new standard for national emergencies.

The Supreme Court agreed that the Constitution imposed no limits on congressional authority in time of war, including the delegation of unlimited discretion to the president. "[T]he complete and undivided character of the war power of the United States is not disputable," a unanimous Court ruled in 1919. Not even the Bill of Rights was sacrosanct. The first test came with passage of the Espionage Acts of 1917 and 1918. These measures imposed a postal censorship of treasonable and seditious materials, made it a felony to obstruct enlistment or incite mutiny in the armed forces, and forbade any disloyal speech or publication. They clearly were aimed at silencing individuals who opposed the war.

When persons convicted under the acts appealed, the Supreme Court adopted what was known as the "bad tendency test," a standard borrowed from common law. Freedom of speech and press meant only that government could not censor speech or press, a doctrine known as "no prior restraint." Speech or writing that tended to produce an unlawful act was not protected, such as when falsely yelling fire in a crowded theater. The "clear and present danger" test became the standard formulation because, as

Justice Oliver Wendell Holmes Jr., wrote, "many things that might be said in time of peace are such hindrance to [a nation's] effort that their utterance will not be endured."

The broad assertion of presidential power and congressional acquiescence became even more pronounced in World War II. The Supreme Court already had accepted the vast expansion of federal power in a national emergency, although enhanced executive power still depended on congressional approval. A case in 1936, however, dramatically changed this formula. Congress authorized President Franklin D. Roosevelt to embargo arms shipments to countries at war in South America, which an arms supplier challenged as an unconstitutional delegation of power. The Court disagreed. It affirmed the "plenary and exclusive power of the President as the sole organ of the federal government in foreign affairs—a power which does not require as a basis for its exercise an act of Congress" (*United States v. Curtiss-Wright Export Corporation*, 1936). The decision became a cornerstone of unprecedented executive authority in foreign affairs, which inevitably meant matters of war and peace.

The arrival of World War II made the implications of this doctrine apparent. By 1940 President Franklin D. Roosevelt became convinced that Adolf Hitler's Third Reich endangered America's national security. Despite an isolationist Congress and public, Roosevelt vigorously used presidential power to support the Allied cause. He ignored a legislative ban and authorized the exchange of fifty over-age naval destroyers with Great Britain for leases to British bases in the Caribbean, which Congress subsequently confirmed. The next year he announced an Atlantic Charter that was, in effect, a military alliance with Britain.

To bolster the legitimacy of this and other actions, Roosevelt proclaimed a limited national emergency in 1939 and an unlimited one in 1941. Although the constitutional authority for these proclamations was unclear, they activated a long list of presidential powers that Congress already had granted. Roosevelt felt no need to justify his actions; he believed, as did Presidents Lincoln and Wilson before him, in the president's inherent authority to do whatever was necessary in a national crisis. This power was unlimited, Roosevelt told Congress in 1942, although after the crisis ended, he pledged, these extraordinary powers would revert to the people. It was a breath-taking assertion of authority. It assumed that presidential ability to act in the nation's defense knew no constitutional limits during wartime.

The Supreme Court, as in earlier conflicts, did not interfere; even in dissenting opinions, justices acknowledged the dire situation the nation faced and the general principle that the government could wield awesome powers in responding to the emergency. Few people disagreed. The nation accepted the judgment of its elected leaders that the Constitution imposed no restraints on the effort required to defeat Nazi Germany and Imperial Japan.

The Court supported Roosevelt's actions as commander-in-chief even when doing so placed the justices in an awkward position. In 1942, for example, it accepted Roosevelt's insistence that eight captured Nazi saboteurs, including one who claimed to be a naturalized American citizen, would be tried in military courts even though civilian courts were open. Six were subsequently executed, well before the Court released its unanimous opinion asserting the right of judicial review but accepting the president's actions under his powers as commander-in-chief. Civil libertarians criticized the decision, but it received broad public support and quickly became forgotten until the attacks of 9/11 resurrected the decision as a justification for the government's efforts to try unlawful combatants in military tribunals created by executive order.

Public opinion also overwhelmingly supported the effective suspension of the Bill of Rights, at least for individuals whose loyalty was in doubt. In February 1942 President Roosevelt issued

Executive Order 9066, requiring the segregation and confinement of Japanese Americans and resident Japanese aliens on the West Coast. Fed by wartime hysteria, the relocation program was a patent denial of due process, yet in 1944 the Supreme Court upheld it, citing military necessity.

The same conclusion was not true for civil liberties in general, which fared somewhat better than in either the Civil War or World War I. Nazi tyranny made the conflict appear more a crusade for democracy and liberty than a battle for empire. The Court too had begun its swing toward a greater protection for individual liberty. As a result, most civil liberties cases decided during World War II were more solicitous of individual freedoms than had been the case in earlier wars. Religious liberty, for example, benefitted from a revival of the clear-and-present-danger test, as the flag-salute cases involving the Jehovah's Witnesses demonstrated. Censorship was common, but no longer were civil liberties held in suspension during the crisis.

World War II had barely ended when the United States entered the Cold War. The world quickly became divided between competing ideologies, democracy and communism. Nuclear weapons made the conflict more than ideological and Americans felt tremors everywhere—across Europe, in Asia and Africa, and in the Western Hemisphere. Most ominously, the menace seemed to exist in the United States itself, evidenced by spy rings and theft of military secrets. The threat was real, but the degree of danger and the consequences were unknown, which only made them more frightening. The result was a state of perpetual war, this time against an enemy armed and visible yet also secretive and surreptitious.

The Cold War had important implications for American constitutionalism. For the first time, most Americans believed that peace required a large military establishment—unlike previous wars, the United States did not disarm after World War II—and a defense industry capable of supplying its needs. Both required an expansive federal bureaucracy to manage them. The Supreme Court's acceptance of congressional authority to govern the economy and presidential power to protect the nation in an emergency continued to serve as constitutional touchstones, as did the Court's newfound respect for the Bill of Rights. The trumpeting of freedom and individual rights were powerful elements in the propaganda crusade against Soviet-style dictatorship, just as they were against Nazi Germany. The Court's affirmation of civil rights for African Americans was an element in this narrative, which explains in part its acceptance, the South notwithstanding, by a nation long accustomed to segregation.

Rights claims faced limits when they were thought to threaten national security, even if the harm was imagined or exaggerated. In the late 1940s, the House Un-American Activities Committee (HUAC) staged a series of highly controversial, dramatic hearings trying to show that communist infiltrators had pervaded American life. In 1950 Senator Joseph R. McCarthy (R-Wisconsin) charged the State Department with harboring Communist Party members. The resulting Red Scare spurred witch hunts and blacklists in government, defense industries, education, and entertainment. The Supreme Court consequently upheld the conviction of American Communist Party leaders for conspiring to overthrow the government because they urged workers to read Marx and Engels. Soon, governments at all levels required loyalty oaths from employees and students at state colleges and universities.

The fright ended in the mid-1950s, with the televised exposure of Senator McCarthy's bullying tactics and his subsequent censure by the Senate. The ensuing turn in public opinion made it easier for the Warren Court to limit or reverse the more conservative decisions of the previous decade, ruling that communists could not be prosecuted for merely advocating revolution. By the 1960s the justices banned loyalty oaths in a series of cases, and in 1968 they concluded that the First Amendment even protected advocacy of a violent overthrow except in cases that led to "imminent lawless action." Rights and security also were in play during the Vietnam War when the government sought to stop the *New York Times* from publishing the so-called Pentagon Papers, top-secret documents about the origin and conduct of the war. The Court sided with the paper, deciding that the government had not met the high standard of imminent harm required for prior restraint.

The twentieth century had produced an implicit constitutional bargain. Beginning in the 1930s, Americans demonstrated a willingness to accept a more powerful central government in exchange for economic security and protection of their lives and their rights. This bargain led to a rapidly expanding administrative state to ensure these outcomes, which, in turn, shifted more power to the executive branch.

To accommodate rapidly changing conditions, Congress granted ever-broader discretionary authority to the president. By the late 1940s, statutes commonly included permissive language allowing the president to change priorities, defer spending, and take other actions to achieve legislative objectives. When combined with the president's acknowledged leadership of foreign affairs, the discretionary authority led to a new conception of the office itself. A menacing world and an uncertain economy, analysts and pundits argued, required a strong, vigorous presidency; the executive was not a danger to liberty and democracy but its savior. Not everyone agreed—conservatives, for instance, warned about an unbridled presidency—but even the adoption of the Twenty-Second Amendment (1951), limiting the president to two terms in office, did not slow the shift of power to the Oval Office.

The Supreme Court generally gave a wide berth to presidential responsibility in war and foreign relations, especially when the actions were cast as an obligation under a treaty. President Truman committed troops to fight in Korea without a declaration of war, calling it a police action authorized by the United Nations treaty. Presidents Eisenhower, Kennedy, and Johnson sent troops and advisors to the Dominican Republic, Vietnam, and the Middle East under similar claims. But the Court balked when the president sought to assert control over domestic policies affecting national security. In 1952, the justices rejected Truman's seizure of the nation's steel mills to ensure continued production during the Korean War, with a slim majority concluding that the emergency did not warrant the seizure. This rebuke still left the president with significant discretion in matters of war and peace, which most Americans accepted as a constitutional necessity.

Vietnam and Watergate changed this perception. Beginning in the 1950s, three consecutive presidents sent troops to Southeast Asia in a futile effort to block a communist takeover in Vietnam. By 1968, public opinion turned sharply against the war, with the victorious Republican presidential candidate, Richard M. Nixon, pledging to end the conflict. Nixon instead sent more troops to Vietnam and authorized a massive bombing campaign to force North Vietnam to negotiate peace terms. Two years later, on his own authority, he secretly invaded a neutral Cambodia in pursuit of the Vietcong. These actions met stiff opposition, but Nixon's overwhelming reelection in 1972 persuaded Congress not to interfere with his conduct of the war.

This stance changed when Nixon became implicated in the Watergate affair, a domestic scandal that weakened his political support. Congressional hearings soon followed, probing not only Watergate but also the extent of unilateral war-making by the executive. The War Powers Resolution of 1973, passed over Nixon's veto, sought to ensure a "collective judgment" between Congress and the White House regarding the use of armed forces. The president was required, if possible, to consult Congress before committing troops and to inform both houses within forty-eight hours otherwise. If Congress withheld its consent, the president had sixty days to withdraw the military. Other measures sought to halt the executive practice of covert agreements to further American interests. These steps signaled congressional intention to restrain executive war-making, but presidents since Nixon generally have not allowed the guidelines to curtail their actions.

An expansive war power was one of many claims of executive prerogatives that led to charges in the 1970s of an imperial presidency. The presidential staff under Nixon became significantly larger and more powerful, exercising authority previously assumed by the heads of the various federal departments. Few members of the White House staff had congressional oversight, a problem that became apparent when Nixon repeatedly prevented subordinates from responding to congressional subpoenas. He also claimed the authority to impound money appropriated by Congress and a broad executive immunity for his actions as president. He argued further that presidential power was unlimited except by his own judgment, especially in military and foreign affairs. By this view, he could mislead Congress and ignore rules of criminal investigations when necessary to protect national security.

It was a position he could not sustain. Faced with a demand by a federal district court that he turn over secret tapes that might establish his complicity in the Watergate crimes, Nixon refused. The Supreme Court unanimously rejected his appeal and ordered the release of the tapes (*United States v. Nixon*, 1974). The president was entitled to great deference and even a presumption in his favor, the justices agreed, but he was subject to the law, with the courts responsible for defining the extent of his constitutional authority.

Nixon's resignation in disgrace, the first for a president in American history, checked the growth of an imperial presidency, at least temporarily. Congress became more vigilant in its oversight of executive agencies, most notably the Federal Bureau of Investigation and the Central Intelligence Agency. (Both

agencies had been implicated in the executive abuse of power.)
In 1978 Congress also established a system for appointing
independent counsels, or special prosecutors, to investigate
executive misconduct. For many liberal observers, these actions
marked a necessary rebalancing of power; conservatives believed
the pendulum of reform had swung too far, leaving the president
too weak to protect the nation's interests.

For this latter group, centered in the Republican Party, Ronald
Reagan, who served 1981–87, became the model president. He
was strong on national defense and sought to reverse the
centralization of power at home. His policy of massive military
buildups and a confrontational policy against the Soviet Union
was widely applauded as a catalyst for ending the Cold War. Like
his predecessors, however, President Reagan acted unilaterally in
foreign policy, often leading to conflict with Congress. His
administration's cover-up of its illegal efforts to support anti-
communist rebels in Nicaragua brought public embarrassment
and more congressional oversight.

Concern about the weakening of the presidency after Watergate
led conservatives to propose a more muscular theory of executive
power. Known as the unitary executive, it claimed that the
separation of powers doctrine gave each branch an independent
authority to interpret the Constitution, especially regarding its
own delegated powers. Proponents argued that the vesting clause
gave the president broad and unlimited powers within his sphere
of authority, including the power to resist legislation or other
constraints on his freedom to act.

The unitary executive theory, combined with the president's role
as commander-in-chief, became the centerpiece of the response to
terrorist threats during the presidency of George W. Bush
(2001–09). In pursuing the war on terror, which he described as
new kind of war, Bush advanced new claims to be the sole judge of
his own actions. For example, hundreds of suspected terrorist

were housed at the US military base at Guantanamo Bay, Cuba, where the government argued they were beyond the jurisdiction of US courts but not outside the president's power as commander-in-chief to hold them indefinitely. These detainees also were deemed "unlawful combatants," a designation that placed them outside the protections of the Third Geneva Convention, an international treaty for treating prisoners of war. Guantanamo, in brief, was a law-free zone.

In three cases from 2004 to 2006, the Supreme Court rejected the more extreme claims of presidential power made by the Bush administration. It ruled in 2004 that a suspected enemy combatant who also was a US citizen could not be held without judicial review; on the same day, it held that federal courts, not the executive branch, had the power to decide whether foreign nationals held at Guantanamo Bay were wrongly imprisoned. The justices again narrowed the president's authority to act unilaterally in 2008 by ruling that the Military Commissions Act of 2006, sought by President Bush to resolve the problems exposed by an earlier decision, unconstitutionally denied the right of habeas corpus to prisoners held at Guantanamo Bay. The decision relied upon a series of cases stemming from the US acquisition of Spanish territories following the Spanish-American War of 1898 in which the Court ruled that the Constitution followed the flag and extended limited constitutional protections to residents of these territories.

It is easy to interpret the decisions relating to the war on terror as restricting the president's claim of authority in matters of war and peace—and they do—but it is unclear how much restraint they will impose over time. The election of Barack Obama in 2008 represented a repudiation in part of the Bush administration's more extreme claims but, in fact, Obama continued many of the practices that he had condemned as a candidate. It suggests, at a minimum, the difficulty of reconciling constitutional ideals with conditions in an uncertain and dangerous world, one in which

10. British prime minister Winston Churchill and President Franklin D. Roosevelt meet aboard the USS *Augusta* in 1941 to discuss Allied war aims—before the United States had entered the war. The resulting joint declaration, the Atlantic Charter, exemplifies Roosevelt's exercise of presidential power in the name of national security and contrary to the wishes of an isolationist Congress and public.

military action may not wait for the congressional approval the founding generation thought necessary in a republic.

More than any other circumstance, the state of continual war poses the greatest challenge to the framers' Constitution. The founding generation assumed that the division and restraint of power was the greatest protection for the people's rights, and that, properly hedged, power in government could be trusted to foster liberty. War has always tested this belief, and few presidents have been content with restrictions on their power when the nation's security is at stake. Today, the risks facing the now-powerful United States could scarcely have been imagined in the eighteenth century. And yet it is doubtful that the delegates to the Constitutional Convention would have agreed that unrestrained power is the solution to the problems of security. They too lived in a world of great insecurity. War was ever-present, and it was even more worrisome because the new republic was demonstrably weak when measured against the great powers of the day. For these revolutionaries, war created an emergency but not an excuse. The founding generation did not sacrifice liberty for security, and they trusted that future generations would find the way to preserve this constitutional legacy, even in an age of constant war and terror.

Epilogue: The future Constitution

The United States does not operate today under the Constitution ratified in 1788 or the Constitution as completed by the Bill of Rights in 1791 or even the one revised by the Reconstruction amendments. Nor is it the same nation. The United States, then a plural noun and now a collective one, has grown from thirteen states hugging the Atlantic seaboard to fifty states spread across a continent and beyond. It has experienced a civil war that ended one social and political regime and ultimately ushered in another far different from anything most people could have imagined in 1776 or even in 1865. From its beginnings as a second-rate country with a tiny navy and army, it has grown to become a global economic and military superpower. It is a democratic republic in which democracy weighs far more heavily in its constitutional and societal calculus than the framers would have endorsed. Its citizens vest government with the responsibility for safeguarding their prosperity, health, safety, and welfare in ways alien to the experiences of the founding generation.

As circumstances have changed, so has the Constitution. It is one constant in American history. How this framework for government will evolve is uncertain, but at this writing it is once again facing serious challenges to its revolutionary legacy. Endless wars, an aggressive presidency, a gridlocked and hyper-partisan Congress, a sharply divided electorate, economic inequality, immigration, cybersecurity and privacy, and foreign interference in the nation's democratic processes, among a host of other issues, have placed demands on government and on society that test its constitutional values.

Even though the strains on the Constitution may appear unique, the problems that Americans confront are not different in degree from what previous generations faced. The nation has survived more severe threats to its security, whether military or economic, and to its ever-expansive conception of individual rights. But it has done so only because enough of its citizens valued constitutional guarantees and traditions enough to defend them. The Constitution is not "a machine that would go of itself," as poet James Russell Lowell reminded Americans on the document's centenary in 1888.

The risks facing the now-powerful United States could scarcely have been imagined in the eighteenth century. And yet it is doubtful that any of the delegates to the federal convention would have argued that the solution to the problems of security was unrestrained power. They too lived in a world of great insecurity. War was ever-present. And it was even more worrisome because the new republic was demonstrably so weak, at least when measured against the great powers of the day. For these revolutionaries, crisis created an emergency but not an excuse. Its purpose was to defend a system of government that rested always upon the people's consent, for it was popular sovereignty, the creators of 1787 recognized, that offered the only sure defense of liberty.

The Constitution does not mean now what it did in its first expression. It is not a legal straitjacket, nor is it a timeless framework for government. It is the product of practical revolutionaries who sought to institutionalize radical ideas, popular sovereignty—the people as rulers—chief among them. The framers feared power and they trusted liberty, yet they knew that these two forces would always operate in tension. The challenge was how to reconcile them so the new nation would benefit from both order and freedom. Citizens of the founding generation found the compromise for their time, even as they continued to debate its terms. Ultimately, they trusted that we, the people, would answer for ourselves how best to strike the balance that would further their goal of a more perfect union.

As he often did, Benjamin Franklin, the oldest delegate to the Constitutional Convention, put the issue plainly. At the end of the deliberations in Philadelphia, he noted the carved silhouette of a sun on the back of George Washington's chair. He had always wondered, he told the delegates, whether it was a rising or a setting sun. Now, he was optimistic that the nation had a bright future because it had successfully addressed the issue of power. He declared the carving to depict a rising sun. A few minutes later, as he left Independence Hall, a woman called out to him, "Well, Dr. Franklin, have you given us a republic or a monarchy?" "A republic," he replied, "if you can keep it." How Americans interpret the Constitution during unsettled and disturbing times makes Franklin's challenge the most important one that the United States as a nation will ever face.

References

Preface

Tocqueville reference from Alexis de Tocqueville, *Democracy in America*, trans. Arthur Goldhammer (Library of America, 2004), 310. Coolidge quote in "Ceremonies Mark Constitution Day," *New York Times*, September 17, 1923. Tavern keeper quote from Saul Cornell and Gerald Leonard, "The Consolidation of the Early Federal System, 1791–1812," in *The Cambridge History of Law in America*, Vol. 1, ed. Michael Grossberg and Christopher Tomlins (New York: Cambridge University Press, 2008), 519.

The Little Rock case is *Cooper v. Aaron*, 358 U.S. 1 (1958).

Interview with Senator Ted Cruz, NPR News, June 29, 2015 (transcript), http://www.npr.org/about-npr/418600824/complete-transcript-senator-ted-cruz-interview-with-npr-news. Presidential candidate Mike Huckabee, *Fox News Sunday*, May 24, 2015, transcript http://www.foxnews.com/transcript/2015/05/24/mike-huckabee-lays-out-path-to-2016-republican-nomination-amb-john-bolton-talks/.

Brennan quote from William J. Brennan Jr., "The Constitution of the United States: Contemporary Ratification," in *Interpreting Law and Literature: A Hermeneutic Reader*, ed. Sanford Levinson and Steven Mailloux (Evanston, IL: Northwestern University Press, 1988), 13.

The various surveys can be found at http://www.firstamendment-center.org/sofa, and at http://www.pewresearch.org/fact-tank/2014/07/31/americans-divided-on-how-the-supreme-court-should-interpret-the-constitution/.

Chapter 1: The revolutionary Constitution

Madison quote from *National Gazette*, January 19, 1792, published by Philip Freneau, Philadelphia.

Paine quote from Thomas Paine, *Common Sense*, in *Collected Writings*, ed. Eric Foner (New York: Library of America, 1995), 548.

Ramsey quote from Gordon S. Wood, *The Radicalism of the American Revolution* (New York: Random House, 2009), 169.

Jefferson quote in *The Founders' Constitution*, Volume 1, chapter 10, Document 9 (Chicago: University of Chicago Press, 2000), available at http://press-pubs.uchicago.edu/founders/documents/v1ch10s9.html.

Adams's characterization of delegates from John Adams, *The Works of John Adams, Second President of the United States*, Vol. 8 (Boston: Little, Brown, 1856), *24 Jan. 1787: TO SECRETARY JAY*, available at http://oll.libertyfund.org/title/2106/161740.

Madison quotes on Bill of Rights from "Speech on Amendments to Constitution, 8 June 1789," in *Papers of James Madison, Congressional Series*, Vol. 12, ed. William Hutchinson and William M. E. Rachal, (Charlottesville: University Press of Virginia, 1962–1991), 196–197.

Chapter 2: Federalism

McCulloch v. Maryland, 17 U.S. 316 (1819).

Andrew Jackson quote from *Proclamation to the People of South Carolina*, December 10, 1832, https://memory.loc.gov/cgi-bin/ampage?collId=llsl&fileName=011/llsl011.db&recNum=816.

Dred Scott v. Sandford, 60 U.S. 393 (1857).

Abraham Lincoln quote from first inaugural address at http://memory.loc.gov/mss/mal/mal1/077/0773800/001.jpg.

The Slaughter-House Cases, 83 U.S. 36 (1873).

Plessy v. Ferguson, 163 U.S. 537 (1898).

Chapter 3: Balance of powers

Marbury v. Madison, 5 U.S. 137 (1803).

Holmes quote from Oliver Wendell Holmes Jr., *The Common Law* (Boston: Little, Brown, 1881), 5, available at http://www.gutenberg.org/files/2449/2449-h/2449-h.htm.

United States v. Nixon, 418 U.S. 683 (1974).
Brandeis quote from *Myers v. United States*, 272 U.S. 293 (1926).

Chapter 4: Property

Adams quote from James W. Ely Jr., *The Guardian of Every Other Right*, 3rd ed. (New York: Oxford University Press, 2008), 43.
Marshall quote from *Fletcher v. Peck*, 10 U.S. 87 (1810).
Trustees of Dartmouth College v. Woodward, 17 U.S. 518 (1819).
Charles River Bridge v. Warren Bridge, 36 U.S. 420 (1837).
Chicago, Burlington and Quincy Railroad Co. v. City of Chicago, 166 U.S. 226 (1897).
Lochner v. New York, 198 U.S. 45 (1905).
United States v. Carolene Products Co., 304 U.S. 144 (1938).
Black quote from *Ferguson v. Skrupa*, 372 U.S. 726 (1963).
Liberty and property quote from *Lynch v. Household Finance Corp.*, 405 U.S. 538 (1972).

Chapter 5: Representation

The Dorr's Rebellion case was *Luther v. Borden*, 48 U.S. 1 (1849).
Black voter quote from Walter Lynwood Fleming, *Documentary History of Reconstruction*, Vol. 2 (Cleveland: Arthur H. Clark, 1907), 434.
Alabama leader's quote from Alexander Keyssar, *The Right to Vote: The Contested History of Democracy in the United States*, rev. ed. (New York: Basic Books, 2009), 30.
Supreme Court quote on civic unfitness of women in *Bradwell v. Illinois*, 83 U.S. 130 (1873).
Reynolds v. Sims, 377 U.S. 533 (1964).
Bush v. Gore, 531 U.S. 98 (2000).
Buckley v. Valeo, 424 U.S. 1 (1976).
Citizens United v. Federal Elections Commission, 558 U.S. 310 (2010).

Chapter 6: Equality

Garrison quote from *The Liberator*, July 7, 1854.
Accept the shell quote from Donald G. Nieman, *Promises to Keep: African Americans and the Constitutional Order, 1776 to the Present* (New York: Oxford University Press, 1991), 37.

Lincoln apple of gold quote in Roy P. Basler, *The Collected Works of Abraham Lincoln*, Vol. 6 (New Brunswick, NJ: Rutgers University Press, 1953), 168–169.

Brown v. Board of Education, 347 U.S. 483 (1954).

Roberts's quote from *Parents Involved in Community Schools v. Seattle School District No. 1*, 551 U.S. 701 (2007).

Obergefell v. Hodges, 135 S. Ct. 2534 (2015).

Chapter 7: Rights

Christian nation quote from *Church of the Holy Trinity v. United States*, 143 U.S. 457 (1892).

Gitlow v. New York, 268 U.S. 652 (1925).

Palko v. Connecticut, 302 U.S. 319 (1937).

West Virginia State Board of Education v. Barnette, 319 U.S. 624 (1943).

Gideon v. Wainwright, 372 U.S. 335 (1963).

Miranda v. Arizona, 384 U.S. 436 (1966).

Olmstead v. United States, 277 U.S. 438 (1928).

Griswold v. Connecticut, 381 U.S. 479 (1965).

Roe v. Wade, 410 U.S. 113 (1973).

Lemon v. Kurtzman, 403 U.S. 602 (1971).

Chapter 8: Security

Jefferson quote in letter from Thomas Jefferson to John B. Colvin, September 20, 1810, in *The Founders' Constitution*, ed. Philip B. Kurland and Ralph Lerner (Chicago: University of Chicago Press, 1987), accessed October 10, 2010, http://press-pubs.uchicago.edu/founders/documents/a2_3s8.html.

Ex parte Milligan, 71 U.S. 2 (1866).

Complete and undivided war power quote from *Northern Pacific Railway Co. v. North Dakota*, 250 U.S. 135 (1919).

Holmes quote from *Schenck v. United States*, 249 U.S. 47 (1919).

United States v. Curtiss-Wright Export Corporation, 299 U.S. 304 (1936).

Further reading

The best general treatments of the US Constitution include the classic work by Alfred Kelly, Winfred Harbison, and Herman Belz, *The American Constitution: Its Origins and Developments*, 7th ed. (New York: W. W. Norton, 1991) and Melvin I. Urofsky and Paul Finkelman, *The March of Liberty: A Constitutional History of the United States*, 3rd ed. (New York: Oxford University Press, 2011). Good short treatments are Michael Les Benedict, *The Blessings of Liberty: A Concise History of the Constitution of the United States* (Lexington, MA: D. C. Heath, 1996) and David J. Bodenhamer, *The Revolutionary Constitution* (New York: Oxford University Press, 2012).

Interpreting the Constitution

Sotirios A. Barber and James E. Fleming, *Constitutional Interpretation: The Basic Questions* (New York: Oxford University Press, 2007) offers an overview of the various approaches to interpreting the Constitution. Also useful is Walter F. Murphy, et al, *American Constitutional Interpretation*. 4th ed. (St. Paul, MN: Foundation Press, 2008). A strong defense of originalism by its most vocal advocate is Antonin Scalia, *A Matter of Interpretation: Federal Courts and the Law* (Princeton, NJ: Princeton University Press, 1997). An equally forceful case for the idea of a living constitution is made by Scalia's colleague on the Court, Stephen Breyer, in *Active Liberty: Our Democratic Constitution* (New York: Knopf, 2005). David E. Kyvig, *Explicit and Authentic Acts: Amending the U.S. Constitution, 1776–1995* (Lawrence: University Press of Kansas, 1996) examines the amending impulse.

Forming the Constitution

Those who wish to know more about republicanism and the ideology of the American Revolution should consult two prize-winning books by Gordon S. Wood, *The Creation of the American Republic* (Chapel Hill: University of North Carolina Press, 1968) and *The Radicalism of the American Revolution* (New York: Random House, 1993). The best treatment of how these ideas played out as a constitutional matter can be found in John Phillip Reid, *Constitutional History of the American Revolution*, 4 vols. (Madison: University of Wisconsin Press, 1986–1993), and Forrest McDonald, *Novus Ordo Seclorum: Intellectual Origins of the Constitution* (Lawrence: University Press of Kansas,1985). A readable recent account of the Constitutional Convention is Carol Berkin, *A Brilliant Solution: Inventing the American Constitution* (New York: Houghton Mifflin, 2002). Woody Holton, *Unruly Americans and the Origins of the Constitution* (New York: Hill and Wang, 2007) emphasizes the democratic impulses that shaped the Revolution and led to the demands for a Bill of Rights to be added to the Constitution as a condition for ratification. Pauline Maier, *Ratification: The People Debate the Constitution, 1787–1788* (New York: Simon and Schuster, 2010) portrays the rough and tumble politics of the state-by-state debates on adoption.

Federalism

Alison LaCroix, *The Ideological Origins of American Federalism* (Cambridge, MA: Harvard University Press, 2010) offers an excellent introduction to the most innovative contribution of the Constitutional Convention. A good survey of modern federalism may be found in Joseph F. Zimmerman, *Contemporary Federalism: The Growth of National Power*, 2nd ed. (New York: Praeger, 2008). The best guide to the constitutional changes brought by the Civil War and Reconstruction is Harold Hyman, *A More Perfect Union: The Impact of the Civil War and Reconstruction on the Constitution* (New York: Knopf, 1973). Also see Harry N. Scheiber, "Redesigning the Architecture of Federalism—An American Tradition," *Yale Law and Policy Review/ Yale Journal of Regulation, Symposium Issue* (1996) 227–296. Samuel H. Beer, *To Make a Nation: the Rediscovery of American Federalism* (Cambridge, MA: Harvard University Press, 1993) is a masterful survey by a political scientist.

Balance of powers

The best starting point for the doctrine of separation and balance of powers is M. J. C. Vile, *Constitutionalism and the Separation of Powers* (Oxford: Oxford University Press, 1967). The role of John Marshall in asserting national power and establishing the power of the federal judiciary is explored in Charles Hobson, *The Great Chief Justice: John Marshall and the Rule of Law* (Lawrence: University Press of Kansas, 1996). The essays in Kermit L. Hall and Kevin T. McGuire, *The Judicial Branch* (New York: Oxford University Press, 2002), explore the role of the judiciary and its relationship with the other branches of government both historically and in contemporary America. James L. Sundquist, *The Development of Congress* (Washington, DC: Congressional Quarterly, 1981) is a guide to the institutional history and workings of Congress. The classic study of the presidency is Edwin S. Corwin, *The President: Office and Powers*, 5th ed. (New York: New York University Press, 1984). It should be supplemented with Forrest McDonald, *The American Presidency: An Intellectual History* (Lawrence: University Press of Kansas, 1994).

Property

The best brief survey of the Constitution and property is James W. Ely Jr., *The Guardian of Every Other Right: A Constitutional History of Property Rights*, 3rd rev. ed. (New York: Oxford University Press, 2008). Jennifer Nedelsky stresses the central role of private property in the framers' conception of limited government in *Private Property and the Limits of American Constitutionalism: The Madisonian Framework and Its Legacy* (Chicago: University of Chicago Press, 1994). Lawrence M. Friedman, *American Law in the Twentieth Century* (New Haven, CT: Yale University Press, 2002) is a readable guide to the relationship of economic and cultural change to the shifting judicial role during a tumultuous century. Edward G. White, *The Constitution and the New Deal* (Cambridge, MA: Harvard University Press, 2000) is helpful on the critical years under the presidency of Franklin D. Roosevelt.

Representation

Alexander Keyssar, *The Right to Vote: The Contested History of Democracy in the United States*, rev. ed. (New York: Basic Books,

2009) is the best survey of the struggle to extend the franchise throughout American history. Ari Berman, *Give Us the Ballot: The Modern Struggle for Voting Rights in America* (New York: Farrar, Strauss and Giroux, 2015) is excellent on the right since the 1960s. The meaning of citizenship is explored in Rogers Smith, *Civic Ideals: Conflicting Visions of Citizenship in U.S. History* (New Haven, CT: Yale University Press, 1997). Christine Bolt, *The Women's Movements in the United States and Britain from the 1790s to the 1920s* (Amherst: University of Massachusetts Press, 1993) is strong on woman's suffrage from a comparative perspective. Stephen Lawson offers a good survey of the campaign for voting rights for African Americans in *Black Ballots: Voting Rights in the South, 1944–1969* (New York: Columbia University Press, 1976).

Equality

J. R. Pole, *The Pursuit of Equality in American History*, 2nd ed. (Berkeley: University of California Press, 1993) is a superb introduction to the subject. An excellent, readable survey of the struggles of African Americans to enjoy the promise of equality is Donald G. Nieman, *Promises to Keep: African-Americans and the Constitutional Order, 1776 to the Present* (New York: Oxford University Press, 1991). Mary Frances Berry, *Black Resistance/White Law: A History of Constitutional Racism in America*, rev. ed. (New York: Penguin, 1994) is a sharp indictment of how the state and federal governments have used the Constitution to support racial discrimination. Readers interested in the law of gender equality will want to begin with Sandra F. VanBurkleo, *Belonging to the World: Women's Rights and American Constitutional Culture* (New York: Oxford University Press, 2001). Michael J. Klarman, *From Jim Crow to Civil Rights: The Supreme Court and the Struggle for Racial Equality* (New York: Oxford University Press, 2004), is a masterful treatment of the long civil rights revolution in law.

Rights

Akhil Reed Amar, *The Bill of Rights: Creation and Reconstruction* (New Haven, CT: Yale University Press, 1998), offers a provocative interpretation of the nation's constitutional protection of rights. Richard C. Cortner discussed the nationalization of the first ten amendments to the Constitution in *The Supreme Court and the Second*

Bill of Rights: The Fourteenth Amendment and the Nationalization of Civil Liberties (Madison: University of Wisconsin Press, 1981). The essays in David J. Bodenhamer and James W. Ely Jr., *The Bill of Rights in Modern America*, rev. ed. (Bloomington: Indiana University Press, 2008), explore the contemporary meaning of many of the rights guaranteed by the first ten amendments. David J. Bodenhamer traces the history and modern application of twenty-three individual rights in *Our Rights* (New York: Oxford University Press, 2007); he also surveys the origins and development of criminal due process in *Fair Trial: Rights of the Accused in American History* (New York: Oxford University Press, 1993).

Security

Charles A. Lofgren, "War-Making under the Constitution: The Original Understanding," *Yale Law Journal* 81 (1971–1972): 672–702, is a good introduction to the thinking of the framers. The standard work on presidential war power is Louis Fisher, *Presidential War Power*, 2nd rev. ed. (Lawrence: University Press of Kansas, 2004); a more critical survey is Peter Irons, *War Power: How the Imperial Presidency Hijacked the Constitution* (New York: Henry Holt, 2003). The Civil War and civil liberties is expertly discussed in Daniel Farber, *Lincoln's Constitution* (Chicago: University of Chicago Press, 2003). Robert Higgs, *Crisis and Leviathan: Episodes in the Growth of American Government* (New York: Oxford University Press, 1987) examines how war and economic crises have led to the expansion of national government. The essays in Mark Tushnet, ed., *The Constitution in Wartime: Beyond Alarmism and Complacency* (Durham, NC: Duke University Press, 2005), examines the trade-off between security and rights during periods of national threat.

Index

Index